Business to Business

Englische Geschäftskorrespondenz und Bürokommunikation

Zusatzqualifikation Englisch für kaufmännische Auszubildende

von
Andrea Eder-Panev
Oliver Frank
Ulrike Küppers
Bettina Raddatz
Marielle Süßer-Kautz

Ernst Klett Verlag
Stuttgart · Leipzig · Dortmund

So arbeiten Sie mit Business to Business

STARTER

Thematischer Einstieg ins Thema

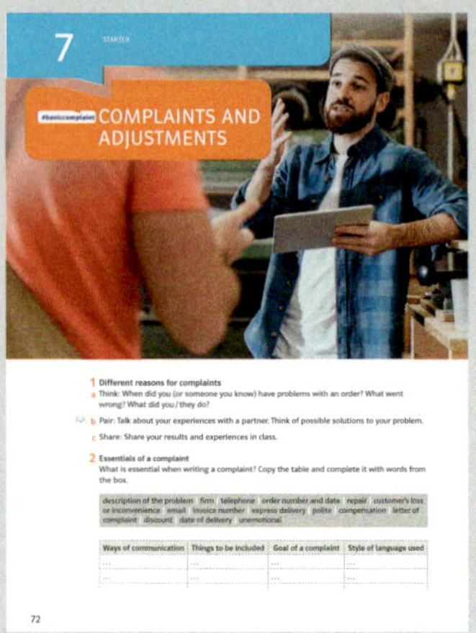

WORKSHOP

Aufgaben für die zielgerichtete Prüfungsvorbereitung

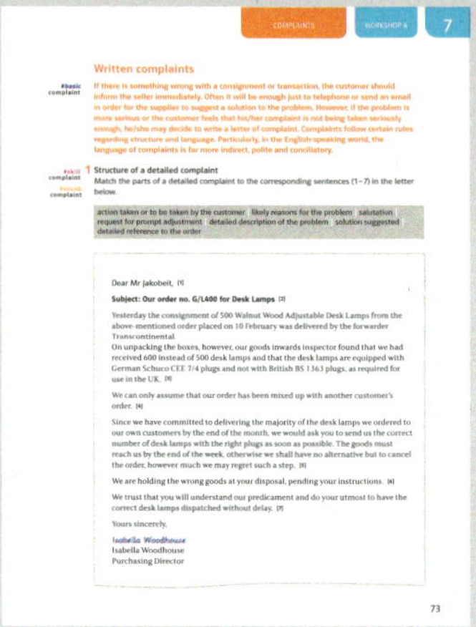

BUSINESS SCENARIO

Anwendung des Gelernten in einer komplexen, authentischen Handlungssituation aus dem Berufsleben

REVIEW

Impulse zur Reflexion des Lernprozesses

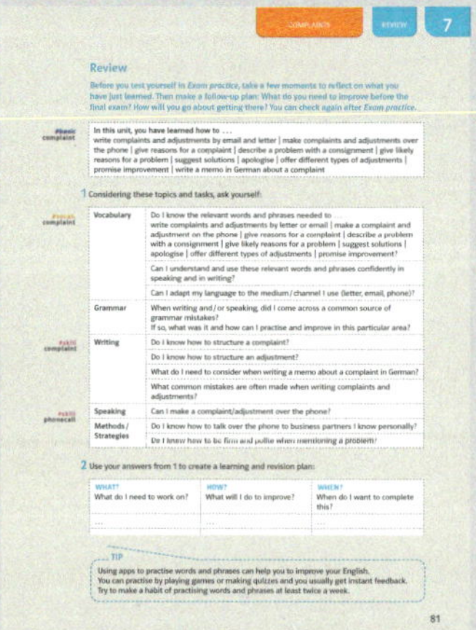

EXAM PRACTICE

Musterprüfungen zum Training zentraler Prüfungsformate

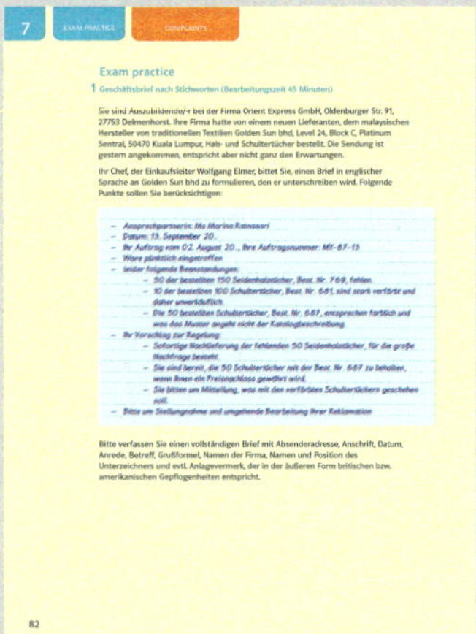

Verweise auf das Basiswissen

Im Basiswissen finden Sie umfangreiche Informationen zu einzelnen Inhalten der Lektionen. Diese Hashtag-Verweise sind thematisch in die Bereiche Business, Skills, Grammatik und Vokabular unterteilt.

So gehen Sie vor:
1. Basiswissen öffnen
2. Hashtag im Suchfeld eingeben
3. Passende Inhalte finden:

BUSINESS BASICS

#basic introducing

Introductions

Essentials

In English-speaking countries, first naming is widespread. When introducing themselves, people often only give their first name. In more formal contexts, they may give both their first name and their surname. As soon as you're introduced, you will be addressed with and referred to by your first name. Never just give your surname, as is frequently done in Germany, as this will make the whole interaction slightly embarrassing – people will not have the option to call you by your first name.

If you want to introduce someone else, you can simply say: *"This is …"* or *"I'd like you to meet …"*. If there's a possibility they might already know each other, you say: *"Have you*

SKILLS

#skillemail

Emails

Business emails have, in most cases, replaced the original business letters. A great deal of today's business communication is done via email because it's one of the most efficient means of communication: emails are quick, convenient and easily traceable. However, they can only be efficient if they are written correctly.

GRAMMAR

#gramifclauses

If-clauses

There are three main types of if-clauses (or conditional sentences) in English. They are basically used in the same way as conditional sentences in German. You can put the if-clause at the beginning or at the end of the sentence.

VOCABULARY

#vocabenquiry

Enquiries

Mentioning the source of address	
Your company / products / services has / have been recommended to us by …	*Ihre Firma / Produkte / Dienstleistungen wurde / n uns von … empfohlen.*

Symbole

Partnerarbeit

Gruppenarbeit

A Audio

V Video

I interaktiv

D Dokument

Alle Audios, Videos, interaktive Übungen und Dokumente zum Schulbuch finden Sie in den Medien zum Schulbuch und im eBook.

1 INTRODUCTIONS

2 ENQUIRIES

3 OFFERS

4 ORDERS

5 DELIVERY

6 PAYMENT

7 COMPLAINTS AND ADJUSTMENTS

8 REMINDERS

9 MAKING ARRANGEMENTS

10 APPLICATIONS

ANHANG

Grammatik-Erklärvideos und interaktive Übungen

Mit Hilfe von den hinter den Symbolen zu findenen Grammatik-Erklärvideos und interaktiven Übungen können grammatische Phänomene wiederholt und gefestigt werden.

V1 V2	I1 I2	**Talking about the present**	– simple present, present progressive – questions and negative sentences
V3	I3	**Talking about the past**	– simple past, past progressive
V4 V5	I4 I5	**Talking about the present perfect**	– present perfect simple, present perfect progressive – present perfect, simple past
V6	I6	**Talking about the future**	– will-future, going to-future, present with future meaning
V7	I7	**Talking about quantities**	– some, any, every, no and their compounds
V8 V9	I8 I9	**Talking about qualities**	– adjectives, adverbs – comparison of adjectives and adverbs, exceptions
V10	I10	**Talking about ability, permission and necessity**	– modal auxiliaries and their substitutes
V11	I11	**Talking about describing people or things in more detail**	– relative clauses: who, which, that, whose
V12	I12	**Talking about conditions**	– if-clauses
V13	I13	**Talking about likes and dislikes**	– the gerund
V14	I14	**Talking about processes**	– the passive: present, past, future
V15	I15	**Talking about passing on information**	– reported speech

1 STARTER

#basicintroducing INTRODUCTIONS

1 Discuss with a partner:

- Where and when do you usually meet new people?
- How do you go about introducing yourself and getting to know others?
- In general, do you feel comfortable meeting new people? Why or why not?

Introducing yourself and your business

#basic introducing

You will often find yourself meeting new people, both in the world of work and in your everyday life. It is important to be able to introduce yourself and your company.

A1

1 Listening: Nice to meet you!

a On the first day of vocational college, Laura, Max and Tarek are asked to introduce themselves and their jobs in English. Listen to their introductions and take notes about their jobs, companies, likes and dislikes.

	Laura	Max	Tarek
Job title	…	…	…
Company	…	…	…
Likes and dislikes	…	…	…

b Work in small groups and introduce yourselves.

#vocab introducing

2 Get to know me

a Collect relevant words and phrases for your own introduction.
- Personal details: hobbies, interests, future plans
- Work details: job training, company, products / services, education

b Use your phone or a tablet to create a 'Get to know me'-video. Work with a partner who can help you prepare and film the video.

! COMMON MISTAKES

I'm ~~of~~ **from** Hamburg.
I ~~am~~ **was** born in Dresden.
I was born ~~on 7 June 2002 in Dresden~~ **in Dresden on 7 June 2002**.
I'm training / working ~~as event~~ **as an event** manager.
We ~~are specialised~~ **specialise** in providing …

TIP

A 'Get to know me'-video is also something you could use for a job application. Sometimes it is beneficial to stand out from the crowd and this might be a good way to do so.

A2

3 Listening: Introducing companies

Listen to these people introducing their companies. Take notes and compare them in class.

#vocab introducing

4

Work in small groups. Brainstorm ideas and think of a business you would like to set up. Come up with a catchy name for it. Introduce your company to the other groups. Consider the following questions:
- What line of business appeals to you? (fashion, advertising, tourism, catering, cycling equipment, …)
- What products or services do you offer?
- What type of company is it? (start-up, chain, family business, global player, …)
- What are some of the different roles and functions within your company?
- Why should customers choose your products or services?

Small talk and visitors

#basic smalltalk

Sometimes you may have to greet visitors at your company and make them feel at home. It may be necessary to make introductions and to entertain them for a while.

1 Entertaining visitors

#vocab smalltalk

a You are Dr Sandra Kaiser's assistant at Minerva International. A visitor, Merete Andersen, arrives from Denmark. She has an appointment with Dr Kaiser. In case Dr Kaiser is delayed, she has asked you to entertain Ms Andersen until she arrives. Role play the situation with a partner.

Ms Andersen	Assistant
good morning	
	good morning / how help?
my name / Merete Andersen / appointment	
	moment, please / ring her / afraid / not answer / not arrive yet / try her mobile / stuck in traffic / here 15 minutes / like coffee / tea / biscuits?
like / tea please	
	order it / how flight?
no problems / on time / only take an hour / slight turbulence	
	first visit / Augsburg? / how long / stay here?
yes / first visit / beautiful old city / just today / return this evening	
	pity / what weather like / Copenhagen?
rain / not warm as here	
	very hot here / no rain / thunderstorm forecast / like Financial Times / while wait?
thank you / have paper	
	Dr Kaiser / here soon
thank you	

b Work with a partner. Make up dialogues using the following prompts. Switch roles.

Partner A	Partner B
flight / trip / journey	pleasant / rather tedious / lots of turbulence / lots of traffic jams on the motorway / long delay at airport
weather	sunny / overcast / slight drizzle / torrential rain / fog / gale-force winds / snow / cold for the time of year / ghastly / brilliant / dreadful / awful
first visit to …	oh no, many times / once before but only for a few hours / no, never
hotel	nice and quiet / service excellent / rather noisy / central / not very central / not convenient for exhibition centre / superb restaurant
interests / sport	prefer soccer / tennis / rugby / swimming / … / support … club

Exam practice

Gespräch in der Fremdsprache – Unterhaltung über Themen des Ausbildungsbereichs (Dauer ca. 10–15 Minuten)

Bereiten Sie zunächst Ihre Antworten auf die unten gestellten Fragen vor.
Üben Sie dann zu zweit. Übernehmen Sie die Rollen **Prüfer/-in** und **Kandidat/-in** und versuchen Sie, eine echte Unterhaltung zu führen und nicht nur ein Frage- und Antwortspiel. Tauschen Sie nach einem Durchgang die Rollen.

Prüfer/-in

Begrüßen Sie Ihren Kandidaten / Ihre Kandidatin. Beginnen Sie das Gespräch mit Fragen zu seiner / ihrer Person und der Ausbildung.	
Good morning / afternoon … Could you introduce yourself, please? Where do you live? Where are you doing your traineeship?	How long have you been working for …? When did you start your training? When does it finish?
Stellen Sie dann möglichst offene Fragen zum Unternehmen:	
Could you describe your firm? Is it a manufacturer or a service provider? What are its main products or services? Roughly how many people does it employ? Does it have subsidiaries or other branches?	Where are its main markets – domestic, EU or overseas? How well is this particular sector doing currently?
Fragen Sie auch nach Details zur Ausbildung:	
Where are you attending vocational school? Are you on block release or do you attend school one day a week? What are your favourite subjects? Do you find vocational school useful in your work? Could you tell us more about your work? Which departments have you worked in? Which did you prefer? Were there any departments you didn't like?	Could you describe your daily routine? In your opinion, how could the training in your company be improved?* Could you describe the dual system of vocational training in Germany?* When are you going to sit your final exam? What are your main subjects? What field would you like to work in when you have completed your training?
Sprechen Sie auch einige allgemeine Themen an:	
What are your plans for the future (work, further training, travel)? Have you ever been to the UK, USA or another English-speaking country?	What were your first impressions? Are you interested in music or sport? What are your hobbies?

*Themen für besonders gute Kandidaten/Kandidatinnen

Kandidat/-in
Beantworten Sie die Fragen Ihres Prüfers / Ihrer Prüferin. Achten Sie darauf, möglichst effizient, klar strukturiert und sprachlich präzise zu antworten: Vermeiden Sie unnötige Ausschweifungen, gliedern Sie Ihre Antwort mit Hilfe von Konnektoren *(first of all, next, moreover, also, …)* wenn nötig in mehrere Abschnitte und drücken Sie sich möglichst genau und verständlich aus. Das bedeutet auch, Fachvokabular aus Ihrer Branche anzuwenden. Reagieren Sie freundlich und höflich.

2 STARTER

#basicenquiry ENQUIRIES

1 Enquiries in everyday life

a Think: When did you (or someone you know) have to find a potential supplier for a product or service (e.g. an event location, caterer, printer, ...)? How did you find the necessary information? What was your experience?

b Pair: Talk about your experiences with a partner. Write down tips on how to find relevant information.

c Share: Share your results and experiences in class.

2 Looking for suppliers at work

a The internet is usually the most convenient way of finding suppliers in a business context, but traditional sources of information are also still used.
Match the sources of information (1 – 4) below with their German translation (A – D).

1 chambers of commerce	**A** Messen und Ausstellungen
2 trade associations	**B** Geschäftspartner
3 trade fairs and exhibitions	**C** Handelskammern
4 business partners	**D** Handelsverbände

b In small groups, brainstorm products and / or services that are needed at your place of work. Where would you find suitable suppliers for them?

Written enquiries

#basicenquiry

Business transactions usually start with an enquiry. There are two different kinds of enquiries. When making a *general enquiry*, you may ask for sales literature (i.e. catalogues, brochures or leaflets), price lists and information about business terms (i.e. terms of payment and delivery, delivery times and discounts). In a *specific enquiry*, you may ask for a detailed quotation or particulars of the goods or services requested.

#skillenquiry
#vocabenquiry

1 Structure of a detailed enquiry

Match the parts of a detailed enquiry in the box to the corresponding sentences (1–10) in the letter below.

reason for enquiry | complimentary close | subject line | request for catalogue and price list | source of address | appropriate salutation | request for information on terms of payment and delivery | closing phrase | further requests (e.g. samples, presentation, demonstration) | introduction of your firm

Sponsorship [1]

Dear Sir / Madam, [2]

We saw your advertisement for racing bikes in the March issue of the German "Tour" magazine. [3]

We are a language school based in Essen, Germany and regularly sponsor sports events in the Ruhr area, mainly cycling and running. [4]

As our sponsorship programme has been a resounding success with local athletes for the past five years, we are now planning to branch out into regional and national events. Therefore, we are considering commissioning high-quality racing bikes custom-designed in our company colours and featuring our logo. [5]

Kindly send us your latest catalogue and export price list, together with minimum quantities for special designs. [6]

Please also let us know your terms of payment and delivery and give us an indication of your delivery times. [7]

Are you planning on exhibiting your products at the ISPO Bike Fair in Munich this year? We would be keen to visit your stand if so. [8]

We look forward to hearing from you soon. [9]

Yours sincerely, [10]

...

#skillemail
#skillenquiry
#gram prepositions

2 Enquiry by email

a Jessica is a trainee office management assistant who is going to do an internship in Dublin. She will occasionally need a car and is looking for a car-sharing company. Complete her email to a company she found with 10 of the 12 prepositions below.

on / about | at | for | from | in | in | of | on | to | to | under | with

From: Jessica Weber
To: CiTee Transit-Share
Subject: Enquiry about car-sharing options in summer 20..

Dear Mr Taylor,

I recently visited your website which lists several car-sharing options. I will be doing an internship in Dublin **1** 1st July **2** 15th August 20.. and I am interested **3** obtaining information **4** low-budget car-sharing options. Could you please send me an overview of the cars available as an attachment and a quotation **5** renting one **6** an hourly basis? How many weeks **7** advance do I need to book? Are there any additional fees to pay as I am **8** 26 years of age?
Please provide me with all the necessary details, including your terms **9** business.
I look forward **10** receiving your reply.

Kind regards,
Jessica Weber

#skillmemo
D3 Memo

b Sie arbeiten für die OfficeTec OHG, einem Großhändler für Computer in Nürnberg. Sie haben eine Anfrage eines schottischen Einzelhändlers erhalten. Lesen Sie die Anfrage und erstellen Sie einen Vermerk auf Deutsch für Ihre Vorgesetzte Frau Arzu Yavuz.

From: Ian McComb
To: Arzu Yavuz
Date: 12th April 20..
Subject: Enquiry about STB 3 and STB 4 monitors

Dear Ms Yavuz,

We saw your advertisement for the STB 3 and new STB 4 monitors in the latest issue of Computer Online and would like to ask you for further details.
We are a chain of retailers for high-end computers and monitors with 10 outlets in Scotland.
Could you please send us a quotation for 200 STB 3 monitors and a sample of your new STB 4 monitor for test purposes? We would also appreciate information on your terms of delivery and payment, as well as any discounts.
Lastly, may we also request your latest catalogue and price list?
We look forward to hearing from you soon.

Yours sincerely,
Ian McComb
Purchasing Assistant | CompuOne Ltd. | 21 Peterson Arcade | Glasgow G69 6AN | Scotland | www.compuone.co...uk

#skillletter
#vocabenquiry
D4 Enquiry

3 Enquiry by letter

Sie haben eine Ausbildung als Groß- und Außenhandelskaufmann / -frau mit der Zusatzqualifikation abgeschlossen und arbeiten bei der in Süddeutschland führenden Warenhauskette Kufstadt GmbH (Turmstr. 15, 86150 Augsburg). Sie suchen nach einem innovativen Hersteller von Haarpflegeprodukten und sind auf Moreale Cosmetics Inc. (255 Montreal Street, Burlington, VT 05401, USA) gestoßen. Ansprechpartner für den internationalen Verkauf ist Chris Peters.
Ihre Vorgesetzte Jasmin Kulzer *(Purchasing Manager)* bittet Sie, eine Anfrage als Brief zu schreiben. Nutzen Sie Ihre Notizen aus dem Gespräch mit ihr.

- *passende Betreffzeile*
- *Bezug auf Internetseiten von Moreale Cosmetics*
- *Vorstellung unserer Firma mit Hinweis auf beiliegende Firmenbroschüre*
- *Angebot über 10 Kisten Moreale TechOne Haargel (TO / 321) und 10 Kisten Moreale TechTwo Haargel (TT / 327) einholen*
- *Bitte um Informationen zu Lieferzeit und möglichen Rabatten*
- *Bitte um Angabe der Liefer- und Zahlungsbedingungen*
- *Nennung von Referenzen in Deutschland*
- *Anfrage angemessen abschließen*
- *Anlage Firmenbroschüre*

4 Types of discounts

Match each type of discount to the correct definition.

cash discount | early order discount | introductory discount | quantity discount | trade discount

1. Your company wants to sell new products.
2. Customers who order well in advance should be rewarded.
3. Customers should be encouraged to pay within a few days.
4. You should grant this discount to retailers.
5. You should grant this discount for large orders.

! COMMON MISTAKES

1. Enquiry ~~for~~ **about** …
2. You have been ~~recommended us~~ recommended **to** us by …
3. We are ~~specialized~~ **specialising** in …
4. A ~~mayor~~ **major** supplier
5. We are ~~interesting~~ **interested** in …
6. An offer ~~about~~ **for** …
7. Please send us a ~~prospect~~ **brochure / catalogue**.
8. We will send it to you in a ~~seperate~~ **separate** email.
9. ~~How~~ **What** are your terms of payment?
10. A visit ~~of~~ **from** your representative …
11. ~~We would be appreciated~~ **We would appreciate it** if you …
12. ~~A soon~~ **A prompt** reply would be appreciated.
13. We hope to ~~hearing~~ **hear** from you soon.
14. We look forward to ~~hear~~ **hearing** from you.

Telephone enquiries

Telephone enquiries are usually the fastest way to get the necessary information about a supplier or a product. In a telephone call, it is often easier to ask directly for special offers. This is especially true if you have already had previous contact with the supplier.

A3 ◁)) **1 Asking for catalogues and prices**

Listen to the dialogue and complete the transcript with the missing words or expressions.

Joan Shedd:	Good afternoon. Wedgewood Promotional Items Ltd, Joan Shedd **1**. How can I help you?
Chris Halter:	Hello, this is Chris Halter from HeyBikes in Berlin. We are really **2** some of your promotional items. Could you send us your **3** catalogue and a price list?
Joan Shedd:	Certainly. Would you like me to send it via email or **4**?
Chris Halter:	I'd prefer an **5**, please. You can send it directly to my boss.
Joan Shedd:	What's your boss's email address? Could you please spell it out for me?
Chris Halter:	Sure. It's **6**. I'll just repeat it: **7**.
Joan Shedd:	Thanks a lot. I've got it. I'll send it right away.
Chris Halter:	I'd also like to ask if you can **8** some promotional items which we could use as a **9** for our new customers.
Joan Shedd:	Well, USB sticks and power banks **10** with logos are still the most popular items after regular pens, of course. Our catalogue includes some very **11** offers.
Chris Halter:	Thanks. That sounds good. We're looking forward to **12** your email then.
Joan Shedd:	You're welcome. Is there anything else I can help you with?
Chris Halter:	No thank you – not at **13**. Goodbye.
Joan Shedd:	Goodbye and thanks a lot for calling.

A4 🔈 **2 Listening to a voicemail message**

You are doing an internship in the sales department of Solarspeicher AG in Rostock. Your company is a leading supplier of battery storage systems for solar power. Mark Fuchs, the head of the department, asks you to listen to a voicemail message and inform him of all the relevant details.

a Listen carefully and take notes about:

1. name of company and contact person
2. products / services the company offers
3. required product and quantity
4. further information needed

#skillmemo
D3 Memo

b Write a memo about the phone call for Mark Fuchs in German.

3 Role play: Enquiry over the phone

#vocabenquiry
#skillphonecall

You work in the Personnel Department of BC Business Consultants GmbH, a large German consultancy firm based in Frankfurt. Your company is planning to send its executives on intensive language training courses abroad. A business associate of yours has recommended Regent School in Edinburgh, Scotland. Role play the call with a partner.

Partner A	Partner B
Identify yourself and state reason for calling. Refer to business associate.	
	Answer the call. Very pleased to have been recommended. Glad to help.
Ask about course offers.	
	What courses exactly? Group or one-to-one?
Mainly one-to-one, but what group courses are offered?	
	Small groups of up to six participants. Can be combined with individual tuition.
Lesson duration? 45 or 60 min?	
	Generally 60 min, from 9 am to 4 or 5 pm. How many students?
Not sure yet, maybe 6 – 10. How many hours per day?	
	Various options, for example 3 hours group and 3 hours individual tuition.
Costs?	
	Happy to send price list by email. Email address?
your.name@BCConsultants…net	
	Thanks. Price list and PDF brochure will be sent shortly.
Thanks for help.	

Business scenario

Sie sind Assistent/-in des Vertriebsleiters Thomas Jakobs bei der MTZ-Maschinenfabrik in Hannover. Das Unternehmen hat viele Kunden aus Großbritannien und den USA. Herr Jakobs hat eine Nachricht in Englisch auf dem Anrufbeantworter.

Step 1
A5

Fassen Sie die wichtigsten Inhalte der Nachricht für Herrn Jakobs stichwortartig auf Deutsch zusammen.

Step 2

Nachdem Sie Herrn Jakobs die Zusammenfassung der Nachricht auf Deutsch gegeben haben, finden Sie auf Ihrem Schreibtisch eine Notiz.

Erledigen Sie die in der Notiz genannten Aufgaben und schreiben Sie anschließend eine entsprechende Mail an Herrn Jakobs.

– Tagesablaufplan für den 23. Juni ab 10.00 Uhr erstellen (in Englisch)
– Freizeitaktivität am Nachmittag in Hannover recherchieren
– Restaurant für Abendessen in der Nähe des Hotels suchen
Mir bitte dann per Mail zuschicken.
Danke
Thomas Jakobs

Step 3
#skillemail
#vocabemail
D1
Email

Schreiben Sie für Herrn Jakobs einen Entwurf für eine E-Mail an den Anrufer und beachten Sie dabei folgende Informationen, die Sie mit Ihrem Vorgesetzten abgestimmt haben.

- *freuen uns auf den Besuch und das Wiedersehen*
- *zeigen gerne die Produktionshallen und die neuesten Produkte*
- *Tagesablaufplan mit Freizeitaktivität und gemeinsamem Abendessen erstellt*
- *Bitte um Rückmeldung, ob der Plan passt*
- *kein Dolmetscher nötig*
- *bei Fragen jederzeit melden*
- *Tagesablaufplan angehängt*

Review

Before you test yourself in *Exam practice*, take a few moments to reflect on what you have just learned. Then make a follow-up plan: What do you need to improve before the final exam? How will you go about getting there? You can check again after *Exam practice*.

#basicenquiry

In this unit, you have learned how to ...
write enquiries by email or letter | make a telephone enquiry | ask about discounts, terms of payment and delivery, delivery times, sales literature, references | write a memo in German about a telephone enquiry

1 Considering these topics and tasks, ask yourself:

#vocabenquiry #vocabemail	**Vocabulary**	Do I know the relevant words and phrases needed to ... write enquiries by email or letter | make a telephone enquiry | ask about discounts, terms of payment and delivery, delivery times, sales literature, references?
		Can I understand and use these relevant words and phrases confidently in speaking and in writing?
		Can I adapt my language to the medium / channel I use (letter, email, phone)?
#gramtenses #gram prepositions	**Grammar**	When writing and / or speaking, did I come across a common source of grammar mistakes? If so, what was it and how can I practise and improve in this particular area?
#skillenquiry #skillmemo	**Writing**	Do I know how to structure an enquiry?
		What do I need to consider when writing a general or specific enquiry?
		What do I need to consider when writing a memo in German?
		What common mistakes are often made when writing enquiries?
#skill phonecall	**Speaking**	Can I make an enquiry on the phone?
	Methods / Strategies	Do I know how to spell correctly and can I take down names / email addresses / numbers correctly?

2 Use your answers from 1 to create a learning and revision plan.

WHAT? What do I need to work on?	**HOW?** What will I do to improve?	**WHEN?** When do I want to complete this?
...	...	...

TIP

Practising on online sites can help to improve your grammar. Usually you will get direct feedback and an explanation of the answer. Try to make it a habit to practise grammar online at least once or twice a week.

A6 2 Vermerk über ein Telefongespräch (Bearbeitungszeit 20 Minuten)

Im folgenden Gespräch sind Sie Pia Poselleck von der Firma City Tours in Hamburg. Sie erhalten einen Anruf von einem potenziellen Kunden aus Birmingham. Verfolgen Sie das Gespräch und fertigen Sie für die Leiterin der Abteilung Bildungsprogramme, Anita Schwarzkopf, eine Gesprächsnotiz auf Deutsch an.

Pia Poselleck	Alan
City Tours Hamburg. Guten Tag.	...
I'm afraid Ms Schwarzkopf is not in today. Maybe I can help you?	...
Certainly. What exactly would you like to know?	...
Yes, that's correct.	...
I'm not quite sure, to be honest. Ms Schwarzkopf has recently changed some of the tours. I'm sure she will be able to give you more detailed information when she's in tomorrow. Can I get her to call you back?	...
Oh, I'm sure she can. Is that 3 pm your time?	...
Yes, we're one hour ahead. Could you give me your contact details, please?	...
Yes, I've got that.	...
Do you have an extension?	...
No problem. I'll pass it on to Ms Schwarzkopf and ask her to get back to you tomorrow. Is there anything else I can do for you today?	...
Yes, as far as I'm aware we do. I'll put that in the memo for Ms Schwarzkopf. She knows all the details and will definitely be able to help you with all your questions.	...
Yes, certainly. I'll do that.	...
You're very welcome. Goodbye now and have a good day.	...

City Tours
Gesprächsvermerk

Für: ...	
Verfasst von: ...	am: ...
Gesprächspartner: ...	
Betreff: ...	
...	

3 Kurzgefasste schriftliche Mitteilung (Bearbeitungszeit 30 Minuten)

Sie arbeiten in der Exportabteilung des Bettwäsche-Herstellers Schlafkomfort Weber GmbH, E-Mail-Adresse: schlafkomfortweber@online...de. Ihre Firma hat den beiliegenden Brief aus Großbritannien erhalten. Ihr Vorgesetzter hat Sie gebeten, diesen Brief per E-Mail selbstständig zu beantworten. Er hat folgende Notiz dazugelegt:

Schicken Sie als Antwort bitte eine kurze, aber freundliche E-Mail an Frau Johnson.
- *Wir bedauern, unserem Katalog tatsächlich aus Versehen eine Preisliste für den Endverbraucher beigelegt zu haben.*
- *Wir schicken die Preisliste für den Handel als Anlage.*
- *Als Mengenrabatt gewähren wir 15 % bei Bestellungen von mehr als 100 Stück und 25 % bei Bestellungen von über 500 Stück.*
- *Die Bavariabettwäsche ist sofort lieferbar. Wir freuen uns auf Ihren Auftrag.*

Schlafkomfort Weber GmbH
Strelitzer Landweg 73
19053 Schwerin
GERMANY

Slumbervale Bed Linen Ltd
27 Shepherd's Drove
High Wycombe
HP11 5XA
Email: slumberwell@outlook...com

Dear Sir/Madam, 15 January 20..

Thank you for your spring catalogue which we received a few days ago.
We are especially interested in the Bavaria Country Style blue and pink check duvet and pillowcase sets.

However, the price list you enclosed appears to list end-user rather than trade prices and contains no indication of quantity discounts.
Please send us this information as soon as possible.

If prices and discounts are competitive, we may be able to place a substantial order.

With best regards,
Lisa Johnson

Lisa Johnson
Purchasing Manager

3 STARTER

#basicoffer OFFERS

1 Offers in your company

a Think: Does your company offer products or services to individual customers or other companies? What types of offers have you come across? Did the offers lead to orders afterwards? Why/why not?

b Pair: Tell your partner what experience you have in sending out and receiving offers.

c Share: Share your experiences and results in class.

2 Types of offers

What type of offer is presented in each of the following situations?

limited offer | offer without engagement | binding offer

1. A producer of office supplies has sent an offer to a new customer and expressly offered a certain amount of stationery for a certain price.
2. A photographer who wants to expand his work into advertising has sent round an offer to take photographs for a number of different advertising agencies.
3. An online perfume shop is offering free delivery to customers who buy more than 50 euros' worth of cosmetics and perfume in the run-up to Christmas.

Written offers

#basicoffer

Offers are either solicited (sent in response to an enquiry) or unsolicited (sent for marketing purposes on the off chance that the individual or company may be interested in the goods or services offered). Detailed, specific offers are often called *quotations*. Offers for work to be carried out take the form of *cost estimates*. A solicited offer should contain all the information necessary for the potential customer to reach a decision.

#skilloffer
#vocaboffer

1 Structure of a detailed offer

Match the different parts of a detailed offer to the corresponding sentences (1–13) in the email below.

details of products or services offered | closing phrase | terms of delivery | attachment | offer validity period | salutation | complimentary close | subject line | terms of payment | reference to enquiry | additional information | prices and discounts | delivery period

From: …
To: …
Subject: Offer for custom-designed racing bikes **[1]**
Attachment: Catalogue and price list **[2]**

Dear Mr … / Ms …, **[3]**

We refer to your enquiry regarding our custom-designed racing bikes and are pleased to submit the following offer. **[4]**

We can offer you three different types of racing bikes in various colours and designs which can be customised according to your requirements. We also offer a wide range of accessories.
Attached to this email you will find our catalogue giving you more information on our products and designs, as well as the colours we offer. **[5]**
We would ask you to please send us a document detailing your specific requirements, if possible, in eps-format.

For prices see our catalogue and price list. As you would be a new customer to our company, we are delighted to be able to offer you a 2 % introductory discount. **[6]**
Regarding our usual terms of payment, we would expect 50 % upon placement of the order and 50 % upon delivery. **[7]**
Our prices are quoted EXW Copenhagen. **[8]**
Delivery can be effected up to two months after receipt of order. **[9]**
Our racing bikes are transported in heavy-duty cardboard boxes and, depending on the size of your order, also on pallets. **[10]**

This offer is valid until the end of this month. **[11]**
If you need more detailed information, please do not hesitate to contact us.
Although we are not going to have a stand at the ISPO Bike Fair in Munich, a representative of our company will be attending the trade fair and would be happy to meet you to discuss further details.

We look forward to doing business with you. **[12]**

Yours sincerely, **[13]**
…

#skillemail
#vocaboffer

2 An unsolicited offer

The company AB Filter Technology sends an unsolicited offer to Motorenwerke Böblingen. Complete the email with words from the box.

welcoming | provide | deliver | quotation | meet | executed | comprehensive | grant | competitive | brochure | trial | attachment | quality | attention | submit | order | payment

From: AB Filter Technology
To: Motorenwerke Böblingen
Subject: Offer for high-quality filter systems
Attachment: Company brochure

Dear Sir or Madam,

Our company, AB Filter Technology Inc., has over 40 years of expertise in filter and control systems. We **1** professional filter systems at the most **2** prices. The aim of our company is to **3** the requirements of all our customers working in a variety of industries.
We produce high-pressure filters as well as refill cartridges of an outstanding **4**. We would also like to draw your **5** to our new fine-dust particle filters which reduce emissions by nearly 20%. In the **6** you will find a **7** containing illustrations and corresponding technical specifications which should give you a **8** overview of our range of products. We would ask you to send us your precise requirements so that we can **9** an offer for customised products. Upon request, our engineers are also available to provide more information.

You can test out and examine the extraordinary quality of our products by submitting a **10** order for standard samples of our wide range of filters. We usually **11** within a month.

The price of our filters depends on the volume of your **12**. For first orders our terms of payment are cash with order. Regular customers are allowed open account terms. For larger orders we are able to **13** a quantity discount.
We would be pleased to send you a **14** for the quantity and type of filters you need.
Our preferred method of B2B is **15** by electronic funds transfer (EFT).

AB Filter Technology Inc. assures you that your order will be **16** to your full satisfaction and look forward to **17** you as our customers.

Yours sincerely,
Charlotte Heywood
EU Sales

3 Reply to an enquiry

You work for Werbesysteme Frank GmbH, a company that produces digital billboards for a variety of different industries. After receiving an enquiry from an Irish retailer (Patrick Jones from Billboard Inc.), you write a reply informing them that it will sadly not be possible to send them an offer. Use the following prompts your purchasing manager has given you.

- *Anrede; Dank für die Anfrage*
- *Hinweis auf große Nachfrage für diese Produkte und Zusatzmaterialien*
- *deshalb große Knappheit an diesen Produkten (Lieferengpässe)*
- *leider keine Annahme von neuen Aufträgen; Sie melden sich, wenn neue Ware eingetroffen ist, und stellen Lieferung bei neuem Wareneingang in Aussicht*
- *Bitte um Verständnis; höflicher Schluss*

#skillmemo D3 Memo

4 Offer by letter

Chris Peters von Moreale Cosmetics Inc. hat die Anfrage der Kufstadt GmbH erhalten und sendet ein entsprechendes Angebot an die deutsche Firma. Geben Sie Ihrer Vorgesetzten Jasmin Kulzer die wesentlichen Informationen in einem Vermerk auf Deutsch weiter.

MOREALE COSMETICS INC.
255 Montreal Street, Burlington, VT 05401, USA

Kufstadt GmbH
Jasmin Kulzer
Turmstr. 15
86150 Augsburg
Germany

20 November 20..

Offer for TechOne and TechTwo hair gel

Dear Ms Kulzer,

Thank you for your interest in our products and your enquiry of 7 November 20..

Our company has customers throughout Europe and we also have long-standing business relationships with some of the big hairdressing chains in Germany. On our website you can find reviews from customers giving feedback on our products.

We are pleased to submit the following offer for the products you requested:

Item	Quantity	Price per item	Total
Moreale TechOne hair gel (TO/321)	10 cases	$271/case	$2,710.00
Moreale TechTwo hair gel (TT/327)	10 cases	$299/case	$2,990.00
		Total:	**$5,700.00**

Our usual terms of payment are cash with order.
We would like to draw your attention to our quantity discount of 2 % for orders of 30 or more cases of our hair cosmetics. As this is your first order, we can grant you an additional 5 % introductory discount.
Delivery can be effected immediately on receipt of order and will be carried out by air freight. Our prices are quoted CIP Airport Albany.

In case you have not done business with US firms before, we would like to draw your attention to certain formalities which need to be carried out beforehand. As a German importer, it is necessary for you to register for an EORI number, which authorises you to import goods into Germany.

This offer is subject to confirmation. By placing an order, you agree to our terms and conditions. Our current offer is valid until June this year.

We hope this offer meets your expectations and we are looking forward to doing business with you.

Yours sincerely,
Chris Peters
Sales Manager
Moreale Cosmetics

Telephone offers

A telephone offer is very effective to speed up business communication and to make it more personal. With real-time conversations, business partners can clarify possible questions and emphasise certain offers. Compromises can be reached more easily when talking.

1 At the trade fair

As a representative of the German company Elektro Klingenbach GmbH, a manufacturer of professional dishwashers, Paul Rund rings the organisers of the trade fair Eatery in The Hague, the Netherlands. He is enquiring as to whether there is any chance of exhibiting at the fair.

A7 **a** Listen to the telephone conversation and take notes on:

1. customers at the trade fair and which sectors they are from
2. participating countries
3. where to register for the trade fair
4. deadline for registration
5. payment details
6. stand sizes
7. equipment for the stand
8. advertising material
9. catering

Paul Rund	The Hague Trade Fair
Hello. My name's Paul Rund from Germany. I am phoning on behalf of the manager of the German company Elektro Klingenbach. We read about your trade fair Eatery and we are very interested in exhibiting in The Hague.	…
We are a leading company in manufacturing professional dishwashers and related products.	…
Unfortunately not, but we have heard a great deal about this trade fair and thought it would be a good idea to attend.	…
Which countries do most of the visitors come from?	…
How do we register to exhibit at the fair? And when do we have to register? I know the exhibition itself takes place in September.	…
We hope to not only exhibit our products but also to showcase how our dishwashers function. For this reason, we would need a bigger stand. Could you please tell me about the size of the stands as well as the equipment, lighting etc.	…
That's good to know as we have very specific requirements concerning electrical power and water supply. Is there any chance we could publish ads on your website?	…
My last question concerns catering. How does that work?	…
Thank you very much for all this information, you have been most helpful. I would appreciate it if you could send me all this in an email.	…
Thank you again. Have a nice day.	…

#skillmemo

D3 Memo **b** Use your notes to write a memo for your colleagues in German.

2 Discussing details of an offer

#skill phonecall
#vocab phonecall

OfficeTec OHG has received an enquiry from CompuOne, a Scottish retailer. However, the German company still has some questions in order to be able to submit a comprehensive offer. Act out the following dialogue.

OfficeTec OHG	Ian McComb, CompuOne Ltd.
	Answering the phone, Ian McComb speaking.
Sie rufen an und nehmen Bezug auf die Anfrage zu Computermonitoren.	
	Thanks for sending the latest catalogue and price list.
Sie freuen sich über Interesse an STB 3 und STB 4 Monitoren. Weisen Sie auf möglichen Händlerrabatt von 10% auf Listenpreis bei gewünschtem Umfang der Bestellung hin.	
	Most pleased. Question about delivery times of the 200 STB 3 and shipping charges.
Lieferung wird sofort bei Bestellung ausgelöst und dauert ca. 3 Wochen. Hinweis auf evtl. Zölle bei Export nach GB; Preise FOB Hamburg.	
	Doesn't want to pay shipping charges. Wants shipment CIP Edinburgh.
Zustimmung, als Kompromiss, weil Problem bei STB 4: Lieferschwierigkeiten aufgrund der hohen Nachfrage. Alternative: Angebot des STB 5.	
	Disappointed about delivery problems. Question about features and price difference in comparison to the STB 4 model.
Neues Modell STB 5: 50 Pfund teurer, aber interessante Zusatzfunktionen. Kompensation: Einführungsrabatt. Angebot einer sofortigen Zusendung des neuen Modells als Testgerät.	
	Accept proposal of replacement of STB 4. If you are satisfied with it, 20 units of the STB 5 are required in Edinburgh the following month to launch the new monitor campaign of CompuOne.
Hinweis, dass Sie sich persönlich darum kümmern werden. Lieferung des Testgeräts bis Ende der Woche.	
	Question about warranty period of devices ordered.
Garantiezeit normalerweise 2 Jahre, für neues Modell 1 Jahr.	
	Information that CompuOne normally pays 30 days net, 7 days 2%. Ask about your partner's procedure.
Zahlungszeitraum von 30 Tagen. Hinweis auf obigen Händlerrabatt.	
	You need the offer by email urgently.
Sie werden das Angebot sofort formulieren und per E-Mail zusenden.	
	Thank your partner and say goodbye.

Business scenario

Die schwedische Firma Lantbruk AB (Klockargatan 7, SE-12123 Stockholm, Schweden) vertreibt Landmaschinen verschiedenster Art in ganz Schweden. Der deutsche Landmaschinenhersteller Sorglos GmbH (Schwedenstr. 15, 30161 Hannover) ist an einer Zusammenarbeit mit dem schwedischen Betrieb interessiert. Als Auszubildende/-r in der Abteilung für Auslandsgeschäfte werden Sie von Ihrem Abteilungsleiter Robert Bauer gebeten, sich mit dieser Firma zu beschäftigen, um eventuell Geschäftskontakte zu ermöglichen.

Step 1 Auf der Internetseite der Firma Lantbruk finden Sie unter der Rubrik „About us" folgenden Text. Übertragen Sie die wichtigen Informationen ins Deutsche.

LANTBRUK MACHINES SHOP SERVICE ABOUT US CONTACT

Our company is a leading distributor of tractors, harvesters and other agricultural machines in Sweden. In addition to our outstanding products, our company is also well known for its expertise and service which comprises the maintenance of machines as well as the delivery of spare parts. We have over a century of experience in agricultural machines and are in a position to customise our machines to make them best suited for your purposes. With our machines, agricultural work can be made much easier – and with much more accurate results.

Step 2 Die Sorglos GmbH möchte einen schwedischen Verkaufsberater sowie einen Techniker der Firma Lantbruk zu einem Besuch einladen. Ihr Vorgesetzter, Herr Bauer, bittet Sie, bei der Firma Lantbruk anzurufen und die Möglichkeit einer Zusammenarbeit zu klären. Führen Sie das Gespräch mit einem Partner/einer Partnerin. → Role card B, p. 118

Role Card A – Landmaschinenhersteller Sorglos GmbH

- Rufen Sie für die deutsche Firma bei der schwedischen Firma an.
- Legen Sie das Anliegen Ihrer Firma dar (Sorglos GmbH sucht einen Vertriebspartner für ihre Landmaschinen in Schweden).
- Antworten Sie auf die Frage: Vorführung verschiedener Produkte ist möglich. Bieten Sie Gespräche und Vorführung von Maschinen mit den Technikern und dem Verkaufsleiter im Hauptsitz der Firma in Hannover an.
- Vereinbaren Sie für Ihren Chef ein Verhandlungsgespräch, wo Themen wie Lieferung, Service, Bezahlung etc. besprochen werden können.
- Legen Sie gemeinsam Zeitpunkt und Dauer des Besuchs fest.
- Bieten Sie an, die Kosten des Besuchs zu übernehmen.
- Verabschieden Sie sich angemessen.

Step 3 Nach dem erfolgreichen Besuch des schwedischen Vertriebsmitarbeiters in Hannover sendet die Sorglos GmbH ein Angebot für Erntemaschinen an die Firma Lantbruk. Verfassen Sie das Angebot für Ihren Vorgesetzten Robert Bauer und nutzen Sie dazu seine Notizen.

- *Bezug auf den Besuch im Hauptsitz des Landmaschinenherstellers*
- *Angebot für 5 Erntemaschinen Modell EM 23*
- *Verweis auf die Maschinen und deren technische Angaben in der Anlage*
- *Zahlung: 1/3 bei Auftragserteilung, 1/3 bei Lieferung, 1/3 30 Tage nach Lieferung*
- *Lieferung FOB Hamburg, Lieferfrist zwei Monate nach Bestellung*
- *Garantiezeit: 2 Jahre; Hotline für sofortige Lieferung von Verschleißteilen*
- *Gültigkeit des Angebots: 1 Monat*
- *angemessener Schluss*

Review

Before you test yourself in *Exam practice*, take a few moments to reflect on what you have just learned. Then make a follow-up plan: What do you need to improve before the final exam? How will you go about getting there? You can check again after *Exam practice*.

#basicoffer
#skilloffer

In this unit, you have learned how to ...
write an offer by email or by letter | explain inability to make an offer | make a telephone offer | mention terms of payment and delivery in an offer | write a memo in German about a telephone offer | have dialogues on the subject of offers

1 Considering these topics and tasks, ask yourself:

#vocaboffer
#gramtenses
#gram prepositions
#skillmemo
#skillemail
#skillletter
#skill phonecall

Vocabulary	Do I know the relevant words and phrases needed to ... write offers by email or letter | submit an offer by telephone | offer discounts, state terms of payment and delivery, provide sales literature, references?
	Can I understand and use these relevant words and phrases confidently in speaking and writing?
	Can I adapt my language to the medium / channel I use (letter, email, phone)?
Grammar	When writing and/or speaking, did I come across a common source of grammar mistakes? If so, what was it and how can I practise and improve in this particular area?
Writing	Do I know how to structure an offer?
	What do I need to consider when writing a solicited or unsolicited offer?
	What do I need to consider when writing a memo in German?
	How do I express politeness in my letters and emails?
Speaking	Can I make an offer for different items and services on the phone?
Methods / Strategies	Are the phrases I use polite enough for communication in official business correspondence?

2 Use your answers from 1 to create a learning and revision plan:

WHAT? What do I need to work on?	**HOW?** What will I do to improve?	**WHEN?** When do I want to complete this?
...	...	...

TIP

Try to listen to native English speakers in order to find out how they avoid being too direct and how they use standard phrases to be more polite in conversations. Replace negative words with more positive ones.

Exam practice

1 Geschäftsbrief nach Stichworten (Bearbeitungszeit 45 Minuten)

Sie machen eine Ausbildung bei der Leuchtreklamefirma GLOW GmbH (10178 Berlin, Lampenstr. 2). Aufgrund ihrer innovativen Designs und ökologischen Herangehensweise (z. B. stromsparende LED-Leuchtröhren, minimale Verpackung) ist die Firma auf dem deutschen Markt sehr erfolgreich und möchte jetzt innerhalb Europas expandieren. Letzte Woche erhielten Sie eine Anfrage der italienischen Eventlocation Illumina (20090 Milano, Via Delle Rose 2, Geschäftsführer Paolo Santini), die eine Außenwand ihres Gebäudes mit Leuchtreklame gestalten möchte.
Herr Santini bat um ein Angebot zu verschiedenen Designs und Größen sowie Informationen zu Ihren Zahlungs- und Lieferbedingungen.

Erstellen Sie das Angebot für die Leiterin der Vertriebsabteilung, Marion Rückert, unter Berücksichtigung der folgenden Stichpunkte.

- *Bezugnahme auf schriftliche Anfrage mit Details zum italienischen Projekt*
- *kurze Vorstellung Ihrer Firma*
- *Designerstellung digital auf Webseite nach Anmeldung möglich (Design, Größe, Farben)*
- *Entsprechender Kostenvoranschlag auf Webseite*
- *Selbstinstallation oder Installationsservice in ganz Europa mit zusätzlichen Kosten*
- *Zahlung: Vorauszahlung*
- *Zahlungsmethoden: Zahlung per Kreditkarte bzw. Zahlung per Sofortüberweisung*
- *Transport: Paketdienst DHL oder eigener Transport bei großem Umfang*
- *Lieferzeit: 2 – 5 Wochen nach Auftragsbestätigung (abhängig von Standort, Produkt und Versandart)*
- *Überprüfung von Produktions- und Versandstatus im Internet möglich*
- *Garantie: 1 Jahr auf Material, bei Installation durch Technikerteam 2 Jahre*
- *Unterliegt AGBs*
- *Anlage: AGBs, Prospektmaterial*
- *Höflicher Schluss*

A 8 2 Vermerk über ein Telefongespräch (Bearbeitungszeit 20 min)

Das deutsche Einrichtungshaus COSY in Berlin möchte sein Sortiment mit marokkanischen Artikeln erweitern und hatte bereits eine Anfrage an einen marokkanischen Händler gesendet. Um mit der marokkanischen Firma ins Geschäft zu kommen und Angebote einzuholen, bittet der deutsche Einkaufsleiter Nick Kunze Sie als seinen / seine Sachbearbeiter/-in ein Gespräch mit dem marokkanischen Geschäftsführer Zafer Rhinas der Firma Albayt zu führen.

Fertigen Sie für Herrn Kunze eine Gesprächsnotiz auf Deutsch an.

COSY, Berlin	**Zafer Rhinas, Marrakech**
Hello. My name is … and I am phoning from Germany. I sent you an enquiry last Monday.	…
Sorry for interrupting. Could you please spell out your name again? I'm afraid I didn't get it down correctly.	…
Thank you very much. Back to my enquiry. On behalf of our purchase manager, I wanted to talk to you personally to speed things up a bit.	…
I checked your website and saw that you are a furniture wholesaler.	…
We were given the name of your company by a wholesaler in Tunisia. Do you have any other references?	…
We studied your website very carefully and were impressed by your range of products. However, would it be also possible for you to send us your brochures and any other advertising materials?	…
That would be most kind of you. My other question concerns the terms of payment. How would goods normally be paid for?	…
That's great. That's how we usually do business with our other foreign business partners. Can we talk about any possible discounts on your goods?	…
That sounds brilliant. We will definitely take this into account. Another point I wanted to raise is delivery. As you know, the Christmas season is coming up and we would like to have your goods by the beginning of September.	…
Perfect. That's all my questions for now. Thank you for all your help.	…
I certainly will. Thank you very much and goodbye.	…

4 STARTER

#basicorder ORDERS

1 Ordering online

a Think: Have you ever ordered anything online? What did you like about online shopping and where did you come across problems?

b Pair: Share your experiences with a partner. Agree on five dos and five don'ts of online shopping.

c Share: Share your results and experiences in class.

2 Essential parts of an order

A buyer places an order with a seller to receive goods or services. The following three categories should be included in every order. Which information would you expect in each of these three categories? Think of orders sent to / from your own company.

1. Information about the items being ordered
2. Shipping information
3. Payment information

Ordering goods

#basicorder

In business transactions, an order is placed when the conditions of an offer are favourable to both the buyer and the seller. Many B2B (business to business) transactions are made online. After registering with the supplier, a company may place orders via the supplier's website. This method is also widely used in B2C (business to consumer) transactions.

1 Structure of a detailed order

Match the different parts of a detailed order to the corresponding sentences (1–11) in the letter below.

complimentary close | salutation | request for order confirmation | terms of payment | prices and discounts | reference to offer | appropriate ending | terms of delivery and delivery time | description, quantity of articles | subject line | instructions on packing (transportation, insurance, delivery)

Order for raincoats [1]

Dear Mrs Martens, [2]

Thank you very much for your offer of 14 March 20... [3]
As the goods meet with our approval, we would like to place an order for the following outdoor clothing on the terms stated in your quotation.

Article No.	Description	Colour / Pattern	Qty	Unit price	Subtotal	[4]
R12	raincoat	dotted	40	$45.00	$1,800.00	
R14	raincoat	neon light	50	$45.00	$2,250.00	
H14	headband	dotted	50	$6.00	$300.00	
H12	headband	neon light	50	$6.00	$300.00	
				Subtotal	$4,650.00	
				Trade discount 5%	$232.50	
				Total	**$ 4,417.50**	

We appreciate your granting a trade discount of 5% on the list prices. [5]

As agreed over the phone, we would like each garment to be packed in its own reusable cloth bag. It is our mission to supply our customers with sustainable and long-lasting goods and we require all packaging to be plastic-free. [6]

Prices are quoted DAP Flensburg warehouse with a delivery time of two weeks after receipt of order, as you assured us the goods can be delivered ex-stock. The goods must reach us by 10 April at the latest, and we reserve the right to cancel the order after that date. We would also ask you to email us the tracking number once the goods leave your warehouse. [7]
Payment will be made by bank transfer to your account with Palmer Bank within 7 days of receipt of order. [8]
Please acknowledge this order in writing and inform us once our goods have been dispatched. [9]

We look forward to receiving these products as soon as possible. [10]
Yours sincerely, [11]
...

2 Types of orders

a Match the different types of orders to the correct definition.

orders on call | standing orders | trial orders | repeat orders

1. … are placed for a small quantity to test the products or service first.
2. … cover the goods or services ordered previously.
3. … ensure that identical quantities are supplied at regular intervals.
4. … , i.e. orders placed for large quantities called for at irregular intervals, play an important role within the concept of just-in-time delivery.

b Which order would you place in the following situations? Use the terms from exercise a.

1. A window supplier has agreed to deliver different-sized windows to a building company working on a skyscraper. The complete order quantity will be bought within 12 months.
2. A university library gets a new issue of a journal series as soon as it comes out each month.
3. A furniture factory had previously ordered ceramic handles for its kitchens from a supplier. They would need to order more handles to be able to go on with the production.
4. You work for an advertising company and you need prints on a regular basis. The quality of different printing companies differs greatly so you should really test their services first.

#skillemail
#vocaborder

3 Placing a trial order

After receiving an unsolicited offer from AB Filter Technology in the UK, Motorenwerke Böblingen want to place a trial order for filters and cartridges.
Complete the letter below with words and phrases from the box.

Delivery time | Description | Guarantee period | Payment will be made | Terms of delivery | this order is executed to our full satisfaction | We have carefully considered your offer | We would ask you to make sure | Payment | Price

Dear Ms Heywood,

1 and would now like to place a trial order as follows:

Quantity	2	Specification	3
1 unit	high-pressure filter	unit type SF 03	GBP 705.00
1 unit	refill cartridge	unit type SF 10	GBP 137.00

We would ask you to deliver the items on the terms stated below.
4 : approx. 1 month
5 : EXW Birmingham
6 : 30 days net
7 : 12 months for the filter unit
8 by electronic fund transfer (EFT).
9 that the articles are packed with the utmost care.

We intend to do further business with you if 10 .

Best regards,
Mark Eggensperger
Mark Eggensperger
Purchasing Manager Engineering

#skillemail
D1 Email

4 Placing a standing order

The online company Speeder GmbH wants their images edited professionally and they intend to employ the services of the Indian company Image Ltd.
Write an email to place a standing order and include the following notes.

- *Dank für die Durchführung des Testauftrags und Zusendung der Arbeitsmuster*
- *Auftrag: Hintergrundentfernung; Bildformate jpeg bzw. png*
- *Preis pro Bild 5 Cent, Video von 30 Sekunden 50 Cent; Annahme des Mengenrabatts von 5 % bei 100 Bildern und 50 Videos wie im Angebot erwähnt*
- *Frist: Bild- und Videobearbeitung 2 Tage (48 Stunden) nach Auftragseingang*
- *Bezahlung erfolgt durch Banküberweisung bei Wareneingang*
- *Bitte um Bestätigung dieses Auftrags*
- *Ansprechpartnerin für weitere Fragen: Frau Sorglos, Speeder GmbH*

A 9

5 Listening: Improving order management systems

Listen to the podcast and answer the questions.

1. What are the advantages of a modern order management system?
2. When should you dispatch goods to your customer?
3. What are two benefits of clearly stating the terms of payment?
4. What are the advantages of using tracking numbers?
5. What additional costs do you need to be aware of if shipping outside of the EU?
6. What do you have to consider when deciding on a shipping company?

A 10
#skillmemo
D3 Memo

6 Changing an order

Norton Singh, IT manager of a big hotel in Singapore, wants to purchase robots for various tasks around the hotel from the German company Robo KG in Wiesbaden. Mr Singh has already been to Wiesbaden to see Cleany, the hotel robot, in action and has received an offer from Robo KG. However, some changes are necessary before the order can be placed. Listen to the voicemail from Mr Singh and, in a memo in German, note down any relevant information for the Robo KG head of sales, Patrick Bott.

#skillletter
#skillorder
D2 Letter
D6 Order

7 Order letters

Ihre Vorgesetzte Jasmin Kulzer (Kufstadt GmbH, Turmstr. 15, 86150 Augsburg) geht auf das Angebot der Firma Moreale Cosmetics Inc. (255 Montreal Street, Burlington, VT 05401, USA) ein und bittet Sie eine Bestellung als Brief zu schreiben. Sie hat Ihnen dazu die folgenden Punkte aufgeschrieben.

- *Datum: 28. November 20.. ; Ansprechpartner Chris Peters*
- *Danke für das Angebot vom 20. November 20..*
- *Bestellung: 10 Kisten Moreale TechOne Haargel (TO/321), Preis: 271$ pro Kiste*
  10 Kisten Moreale TechTwo Haargel (TT/327), Preis: 299 $ pro Kiste
- *Gesamtsumme: 5,700 $; Einführungsrabatt von 5 % annehmen*
- *Mengenrabatt wird noch nicht genutzt, da wir zunächst das Produkt auf dem deutschen Markt testen möchten*
- *Preis- und Lieferbedingen wie im Angebot akzeptieren*
- *Zahlung im Voraus bei Erhalt der Auftragsbestätigung; Preise DAP Augsburg*
- *Bitte um Auftragsbestätigung*
- *Bestellung angemessen abschließen*

8 Negotiating the terms of an order by phone

#skill phonecall
#vocab phonecall

Ruhr Sprachschule in Essen has received an offer for custom-designed racing bikes from the Danish company Bikes For You A/S. Before placing an order, Ruhr Sprachschule wants to clarify some points. Work with a partner and role play the conversation.

Ruhr Sprachschule Essen	Bikes For You A/S
Sie melden sich mit Ihrem Namen. Sie rufen im Namen Ihres Chefs, Herr Gärtner, an. Sie möchten den Verkaufsmanager sprechen, den Sie auf der ISPO Fahrradmesse in München getroffen haben.	
	The sales manager is on the phone: Bo Hansen. Thank for call and previous email with details of design requirements and requested logo. Company would like to do business with the language school.
Sie möchten wissen, wie die Lieferzeiten sind. Bitten um schnellstmögliche Lieferung.	
	Only limited number of bicycles in stock. Delivery times depend on volume of order. Currently facing delivery problems with carbon bicycles.
Sie fragen nach Lieferzeit von Fahrrädern mit Aluminiumrahmen.	
	Usual delivery time for aluminium bicycles 2 months. You want to know the number of bikes to be ordered.
Ihre Firma möchte 20 Fahrräder kaufen (Katalognummer 321, grau-blau, Aluminium).	
	You will try to speed up delivery.
Reden Sie nochmals über Liefer-/Zahlungsbedingungen. Kommen Sie zu Kompromiss. EXW nicht akzeptabel, besser CIP Hamburg; Rabatt 5 % anstatt 2 %; nicht Bezahlung ½ bei Auftrag und ½ bei Lieferung, sondern erst Bezahlung bei Wareneingang.	
	CIP Hamburg is fine, as is accepting full payment once the bikes are delivered. You can only accept a 3 % discount.
Bitte um schnellstmögliche genaue Kostenaufstellung.	
	Promise to send all necessary information (price, packaging, shipping) by …
Sie betonen nochmals, dass schnellstmöglich geliefert werden muss. Bei guten Geschäftsbedingungen evtl. weitere Bestellungen.	
	Stress you will do your best to speed up delivery. Say goodbye.
Verabschieden Sie sich.	

! COMMON MISTAKES

1. You have ~~supplied us~~ **supplied / supplied us with** printers.
2. We have received your offer ~~from~~ **of** 6 May.
3. We would like to place an order ~~of~~ **for** handbags.
4. Prices are taken from your ~~actual~~ **current** price list.
5. We would like to ~~make~~ **do** further business with you.

#basicorder **9 Filling in a purchase order**

Special forms are often used for ordering goods or services. They are called *purchase orders (PO)* and must be confirmed by the seller before the order can be executed.
You will find the purchase order from Nova Solar below. After receiving an offer from Solarspeicher AG, they have decided to order some Solar 5 batteries.
Match the different headings of a purchase order form to the corresponding parts (1–14) in the form below.

Seller (name and business address) | Buyer (name and billing address) | Order date | Shipping address | Purchase order no. | Signature (buyer) | Delivery date | Item description | Item number | Price per unit | Shipping method | Terms of payment | discount | Warranty period

Nova Solar | Purchase Order (PO)

1 SB 345
(Please state this number on all correspondence incl. invoices concerning this order.)

2
Solarspeicher AG
Spitalstr. 15
18057 Rostock
Germany

Bank details
Deutsche Bank
IBAN …
BIC …

Seller – person in charge: Mark Fuchs
Buyer – person in charge: Alba Gomez

3 23 October 20..

4
Nova Solar
Calle Maria 25
29013 Málaga
Spain

5
Nova Solar / Nova Sol S.A.
Calle Maria 25
29013 Málaga
Spain

6	7	Qty	**Colour**	8	**Total in €**
Solar 5	solar battery	400	white	€2,500	1,000,000.00
Solar 5	solar battery	300	black	€2,500	750,000.00
				Subtotal	1,750,000.00
				Quantity 9 5%	–87,500.00
				Introductory discount 10%	–175,000.00
				Other	--
				Total	1,487,500.00

Other comments or special instructions:
Terms of delivery: ex works (Rostock)
10 : 3 weeks after receipt of order
11 : 10 days net
12 : by road
Further information: Packing in wooden crates on pallets
13 : 24 months after receipt of goods

Standard terms of payment and sale apply.

Date: 23 October 20..

14 Alba Gomez

Order confirmation and cancellation

#basicorder

Confirming an order reduces uncertainty and is a service that lets the customer know that his / her order has been received and is being dealt with.
Orders can be cancelled by either the buyer or the seller. Reasons for cancelling an order can vary from one of the parties being at fault to any other unexpected circumstances.

1 Structure of a detailed order confirmation

D7 Order confirmation

The German company, Solarspeicher AG, has received the order from Nova Solar in Spain. They are now sending an order confirmation by email.
Match the different parts of a detailed order confirmation to the corresponding sentences (1–8) in the letter below.

acknowledgement of order repeating details (quantity and name of product, price and discounts, terms of payment and delivery) | further information | subject line | salutation | goodwill ending | reference to order | complimentary close | information concerning delivery

From: Mark Fuchs
To: Alba Gomez
Date: 26 October 20..
Subject: Order for Solar 5 batteries / Order No. SB 345 [1]
Attachment: pro-forma invoice

Dear Ms Gomez, [2]

We were delighted to receive your order (no. SB 345) which we would like to confirm as follows: [3]

- Solar 5 batteries: 400 units in white and 300 units in black [4]
- Unit price €2,500
- Discounts: 5% quantity discount and 10% introductory discount
- Total: €1,487,500
- Delivery: 3 weeks after receipt of order, ex works (Rostock)
- Payment: 10 days net

We have already contacted our forwarders regarding the transport of the goods. Each solar battery will be packaged in a single cardboard box. The boxes will be packed in wooden crates and stacked on pallets, with 20 crates per pallet. [5]

As agreed, delivery will be paid for by Nova Solar, i.e. road transport by lorry is to be covered by Nova Solar at its own expense. We will send you an email when your order has been shipped. [6]

Please find attached the pro forma invoice which includes all the necessary details of your order. Alongside the consignment you will receive the packing list, the consignment note and the Certificate of Origin issued by the Chamber of Commerce, Augsburg.

Please do not hesitate to contact us if you have any further questions or comments. [7]

Yours sincerely, [8]
Mark Fuchs

A 11 2 **Confirming an order by phone**

Rahul Khan, sales manager at Guptha Rubbers PLC has received an order from Ruth Bennet from The Bike Factory in Leipzig. He calls her to clarify some questions and confirm the order. Ms Bennet asks you to summarise the dialogue for her colleague in the purchasing department in a memo in German.

Ruth Bennet	R. Khan
Good morning. The Bike Factory Europe. This is Ruth Bennet speaking.	...
It's very kind of you to phone me personally. As you know, we are very interested in the offer you sent us for your hard-wearing tyres. They are just right for our new e-bike, the Solar Racer.	...
Perfect! In our order we quoted DDP Leipzig. I just wanted to check that this is convenient for you as you stated FCA in your offer?	...
And can you deliver in time?	...
How much would that cost?	...
Perfect. I would really appreciate that. I reckon I'll be able to send you the order by the end of this week. Thank you, Mr Khan. It was a pleasure talking to you.	...

#skillemail 3 **Cancelling an order**

Nature Ltd. has to cancel a substantial order for homeopathic painkillers. Read the email and complete it using the phrases from the box.

my sincere apologies | confirm cancellation | at very short notice | any inconvenience | We are terribly sorry | cancel our order | We assure you

From: Signe Scholz
To: James Bordon
Date: 12 March 20..
Subject: Cancellation of order for homeopathic painkillers

Dear Mr Bordon,

1 to inform you that we have no alternative but to 2 for homeopathic painkillers which we ordered on 8 March 20..
Unfortunately, our main customer for this type of medicine has gone bankrupt and therefore cancelled all his orders 3 .
We would be grateful if you could 4 of this order by email.

5 that we fully intend to do further business with your company in the future.
Please accept 6 for 7 this may cause.

Yours sincerely,
Signe Scholz

Business scenario

AEP ist ein führender Hersteller von Hörgeräten in Deutschland und produziert Hörgeräte für unterschiedlichste individuelle Bedürfnisse. Die Firma möchte nun mit 3D-Druckern einzelne Teile eines Hörgerätes herstellen, ist aber noch nicht sicher, ob sie diese Teile vor Ort selbst produzieren oder die Arbeit outsourcen werden. Daher möchte AEP einen 3D-Drucker als Testgerät bestellen. Als Praktikant/-in in der Geschäftsführung wurden Sie beauftragt, diese Angelegenheit zu übernehmen.

Step 1

Im Namen Ihres Firmenchefs Peter Wagner führen Sie mit der US-amerikanischen Firma Sono Inc. Sarasota, Florida, die unter anderem 3D-Drucker herstellt (Verkaufsleiterin Europa: Janice Stevens) ein Gespräch bezüglich einer möglichen Bestellung von 3D-Druckern. Führen Sie das Gespräch mit einem Partner/einer Partnerin. → Role card B, p. 118

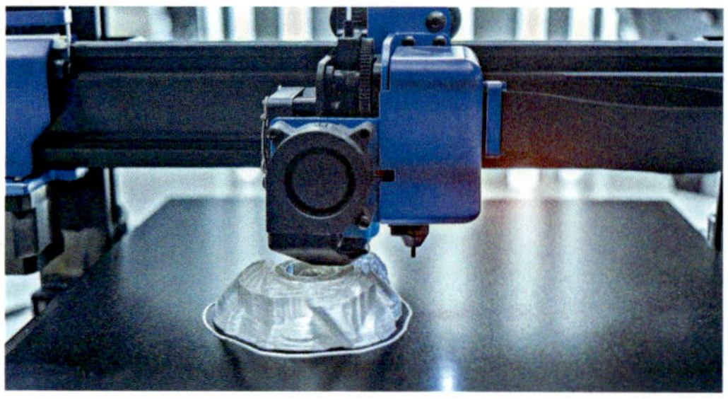

#skill phonecall
#vocab phonecall

Role Card A – AEP Deutschland

- Rufen Sie für die deutsche Firma bei der US-Firma an.
- Fragen Sie nach der zuständigen Person für den Verkauf von 3D-Druckern.
- Stellen Sie Ihre Firma, Ihre Produkte und Ihr Vorhaben kurz vor.
- Ein Geschäftspartner hat Sie auf die US-Firma aufmerksam gemacht, Informationen über die 3D-Drucker haben Sie sich im Internet besorgt.
- Fragen Sie nach den Kosten für einen 3D-Drucker, der für diese Aufgabe geeignet ist.
- Fragen Sie, ob eine Testlieferung möglich wäre.
- Nehmen Sie den Vorschlag die Bedienungseinweisung via Videokonferenz abzuhalten an.
- Kündigen Sie die Bestellung von 20 3D-Druckern an, falls das Gerät den Erwartungen entspricht.
- Kündigen Sie die schriftliche Bestellung des Testgeräts an.
- Verabschieden Sie sich angemessen.

Step 2

#skillorder
#skillletter
D6 Order

Nach der erfolgreichen Testung des 3D-Druckers, hat AEP ein Angebot von der Firma Sono Inc. erhalten. Ihr Vorgesetzter Peter Wagner entscheidet sich für den Kauf von 20 3D-Druckern. Formulieren Sie den Auftrag in einem Brief und gehen Sie auf die folgenden Punkte ein.

- *Dank für Testgerät, hat sehr gut funktioniert, ebenso die Einweisung per Videokonferenz*
- *Bestellung von 20 Stück der 3D-Drucker, Typ 3DP60X*
- *Bedingungen wie in Angebot erwähnt: Preis: 6,500 $, Bezahlung 10 Tage nach Erhalt der Rechnung bei Little Rock Bank, Sarasota, FL, Rabattoption: Mengenrabatt 5 %*
- *Lieferbedingungen: DAP München, Lieferung 3 Wochen nach Auftragseingang*
- *ein Jahr Garantie (kostenlose Lieferung von Ersatzteilen in dieser Zeit), Servicevertrag zwei Jahre gültig*
- *Lieferung von Bedienungsanleitungen für Geräte und entsprechender Software*
- *Bestellung von Druckermaterial erfolgt regelmäßig über PO*

Review

Before you test yourself in *Exam practice*, take a few moments to reflect on what you have just learned. Then make a follow-up plan: What do you need to improve before the final exam? How will you go about getting there? You can check again after *Exam practice*.

#basicorder

In this unit, you have learned how to …
place orders by email or letter | talk about an order and negotiate it by telephone | get relevant information from a telephone call | fill in a purchase order | include different aspects of an order | write an order confirmation | cancel an order by email

1 Considering these topics and tasks, ask yourself:

#vocaborder	**Vocabulary**	Do I know the relevant words and phrases needed to … place an order by email or letter | discuss an order on the telephone | fill in a purchase order | include discounts, terms of payment and delivery, delivery times etc. in an order | confirm and cancel an order?
		Can I understand and use these relevant words and phrases confidently in speaking and in writing?
		Can I adapt my language to the medium / channel I use (letter, email, phone)?
#gramtenses #gramprepositions	**Grammar**	When writing and / or speaking, did I come across a common source of grammar mistakes? If so, what was it and how can I practise and improve in this particular area?
#skillorder #skillmemo #skillletter #skillemail	**Writing**	Do I know the structure of an order?
		What do I need to consider when writing an order?
		What do I need to consider when writing a memo in German?
		What are common mistakes when writing orders?
#skillphonecall	**Speaking**	Can I talk about the different aspects of an order on the phone? Can I solve problems?
	Methods / Strategies	Can I follow instructions on how to do something online?

2 Use your answers from 1 to create a learning and revision plan.

WHAT? What do I need to work on?	**HOW?** What will I do to improve?	**WHEN?** When do I want to complete this?
…	…	…

TIP

Start using more idiomatic business phrases in English by learning combinations of verbs and nouns which often go together. Look out for and expand your knowledge of collocations while speaking to business partners and reading their correspondence.

Exam practice

1 Vermerk über einen Geschäftsbrief (Bearbeitungszeit 30 Minuten)

Sie arbeiten im Spielzeugwarenhaus Zimmermann in Neuhaus in der Einkaufsabteilung. Am 22. Juli hatte das Warenhaus einen Auftrag an die polnische Firma Natural Toys in Kraków, ul. Mogilska 22, erteilt, worauf die polnische Firma eine Auftragsbestätigung gesendet hat.
Fassen Sie für den Warenhausleiter, Herrn Zimmermann, den Inhalt dieses Briefes in einem Vermerk in deutscher Sprache zusammen (vollständige Sätze, keine Übersetzung).

Dear Mr Zimmermann,

We are sending you this letter to acknowledge your order of 22 July. We are very pleased that you have placed this order with our company.
As arranged, further repeat orders can be submitted as purchase orders.

Description	Colour	Model No.	Quantity	Unit price	Total
Wooden car	red	456	20	12.00 €	240.00 €
Dog pull toy	brown	775	40	11.00 €	440.00 €
				Shipping charges	43.00 €
				Total price	723.00 €

The whole consignment will be packed and labelled for shipment according to our usual guidelines. Delivery by post will be executed by 15 August at the latest. The consignment will be dispatched to the address above and we will send you an email once it has been dispatched.

Payment must be made by bank transfer upon receipt of the goods. Please find the bank account details at the end of this letter. Prices are quoted DAP Neuhaus.
We are confident that the products delivered will conform to the specifications mentioned in your order. In case of any damage, replacements will be sent within two weeks.

This order is subject to our General Terms and Conditions.

Please do not hesitate to contact us if you have any questions regarding this order or our wide range of wooden toys. We are confident that our products will fully meet your expectations.

Yours sincerely,
Pawel Woyzak

A12 2 **Vermerk über ein Telefongespräch (Bearbeitungszeit 20 Minuten)**

Das Autohaus Lizzy hat in den USA einen Oldtimer bestellt. Sie nehmen die telefonische Auftragsbestätigung entgegen und sprechen mit Mary Fast von der Firma Vintage Oldies. Verfolgen Sie das Telefongespräch und fertigen Sie anschließend für Ihren Firmenchef, Herrn Gerber, eine Gesprächsnotiz auf Deutsch an. Halten Sie die wesentlichen Informationen zur Lieferung und Bezahlung fest.

Autohaus Lizzy	Mary Fast
Autohaus Lizzy, Olga Meine. Guten Tag.	...
Hello Ms Fast. I hope there is nothing wrong with my order.	...
That's very kind of you. When you pay 15,000 dollars for a car, you definitely don't want anything to go wrong!	...
Yes, I'm aware of that, thanks. I would like the car to be shipped to Bremerhaven, please.	...
Fingers crossed nothing happens then!	...
I'll ask my boss about it right away. In my order I asked you to provide all the necessary documentation for importing the car.	...
Do you know when I can expect the car here in Germany? As you already know, I would like the car to be dispatched upon receipt of order.	...
Is the shipping cost the same as was previously stated?	...
OK. That's a deal then. Please send all these details in your order confirmation.	...
I will do. Thanks very much again. Goodbye.	...

5 STARTER

#basicdelivery DELIVERY

1 Types of transport

a Discuss with a partner how the following items can best be transported. Give reasons.

luxury cars from Cologne to Dubai | urgently needed medical products from Frankfurt to Buenos Aires | construction timber from Costa Rica to Antwerp | steel tubes from Duisburg to Geneva | wine from Bordeaux to Munich

A 13 **b** Copy the grid. Listen to the interview with Malcolm Gledhill of Globalfreight and complete the grid.

	Rail	Road	Air	Sea

Advantages	…	…	…	…
Disadvantages	…	…	…	…
Typical cargoes	…	…	…	…

Trade and customs duties

#basiccustoms

When selling or buying goods and services it is important to consider possible regulations and restrictions. Domestic trade and trade within the EU Single Market are more straightforward than trading on world markets. When buying goods from outside the EU you effectively become an importer and are liable to pay customs, excise duties and VAT. Unless the terms of sale provide otherwise, goods are held by customs authorities upon entry until all duties and taxes are paid.

1 Trade outside the EU

What should a company consider when exporting to non-EU countries? Complete the list using the words from the box. There are two more words than you need.

charges | complies | costly | deadlines | focus | impact | manuals | native | procedures | research

What to consider in international trade:

- For smaller companies it is probably a good idea to **1** on a small number of export markets.
- It is important to do some **2** on the market you plan to target.
- Find out whether your product **3** with local technical standards. Any modification to your product may involve considerable costs.
- Are there any cultural or religious differences that need to be taken into account?
- Sales literature, advertising materials, instructions and **4** need to be translated into the local language. Ensure that the translation is of good quality and checked by a **5** speaker!
- How do you plan to organise transport and deal with documentation? Will you use a freight forwarder?
- What method of payment will you use?
- Large companies will have dedicated export departments. In smaller companies it is essential to have staff with experience of export **6**, including familiarity with export documentation and methods of payment.
- It is essential that documents are completed with the utmost accuracy. Mistakes can cause long delays and be very **7**.
- Keeping to **8** and delivery dates and controlling quality are even more important in highly competitive export markets than in the domestic market.

2 Costs for importing goods

Match the expressions with their correct definition.

charges | customs duties | excise duties | VAT (value added tax) | taxes

1. a certain amount of money paid on goods that are imported
2. a tax on certain goods such as alcohol or petrol raised by a state
3. a tax that is paid by each person when buying goods or services
4. money paid to the state based on one's income
5. amount of money to be paid for something, for example an activity or service

#basiccustoms

3 Customs authorities

a Brainstorm with a partner: What do customs authorities do?

b Complete the text with the words from the box. Then check your answers from exercise a.

branded | cheaply | competitors | copies | domestic | duties | levied | logo | movement | prices | products | protect

Customs authorities

The customs authorities' most important tasks are to levy customs and tax (1) and to monitor the cross-border (2) of goods. So, if goods can be produced more (3) abroad than in Germany, for example, customs duty is (4) on certain goods. This is done to align (5) and protect (6) producers who, for various reasons, cannot produce as cheaply as some of their (7). Customs authorities also (8) copyrights. Companies in other countries often copy (9) goods and want to sell these (10) in Germany. These products are marked with the (11) of the copied brand, although they are made from inferior materials. That is why customs controls also look for counterfeit (12).

c Discuss: What does Brexit mean for the importation of goods?

#basicdelivery

4 Just-in-time deliveries

Read the text and note down the advantages of just-in-time delivery. Can you think of disadvantages and problems of just-in-time deliveries? Discuss in class.

In logistics, a delivery is called just-in-time if it arrives at the customer exactly when it is needed. In principle, just-in-time deliveries offer the advantage that you do not need to find a way to store goods before production. The goods can be delivered directly from the lorry to the production site and can then be used immediately. This process significantly improves efficiency in manufacturing while offering numerous opportunities for cost savings. This, however, requires a sophisticated transport control system as well as a high-performing and reliable IT system so that all parties involved are always kept up to date on important processes.

Packing and labelling

#basicpacking

Suppliers and freight forwarders are responsible for ensuring that goods are adequately packed to protect them from damage, humidity, heat, theft etc. so that they arrive in perfect condition.

1 Are you familiar with these words? Match the English terms with their German equivalents. Look up words you do not know, if necessary.

1 barrel | **2** biodegradable | **3** blister packaging | **4** bubble wrap | **5** corrugated cardboard | **6** coil | **7** crate | **8** cushioning material | **9** desiccant | **10** drum | **11** foam rubber | **12** jar | **13** jerry can | **14** jiffy bag | **15** polystyrene chips | **16** reusable containers | **17** steel strapping | **18** shrink wrapping | **19** stretch wrap | **20** wooden box

A wattierter Umschlag | **B** Mehrwegbehälter | **C** Polstermaterial | **D** Fass | **E** Stahlbandumreifung | **F** Tonne | **G** Styropor-Chips | **H** Luftpolsterfolie | **I** Kanister | **J** Lattenkiste | **K** Dehnfolie | **L** Glas | **M** Schrumpfverpackung | **N** Trocknungsmittel | **O** Rolle | **P** Schaumstoff | **Q** biologisch abbaubar | **R** Holzkiste | **S** Blister-Verpackung | **T** Wellpappe

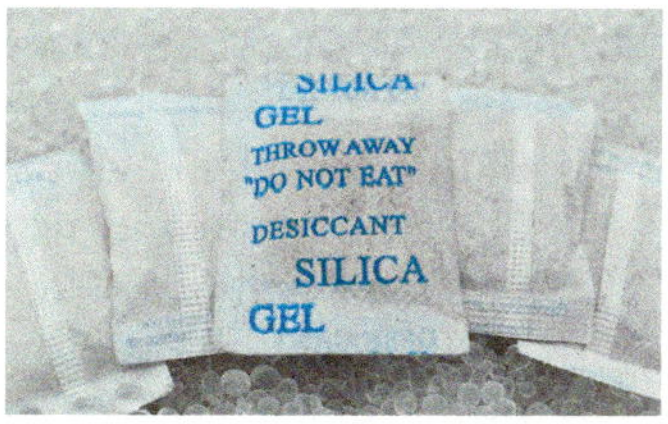

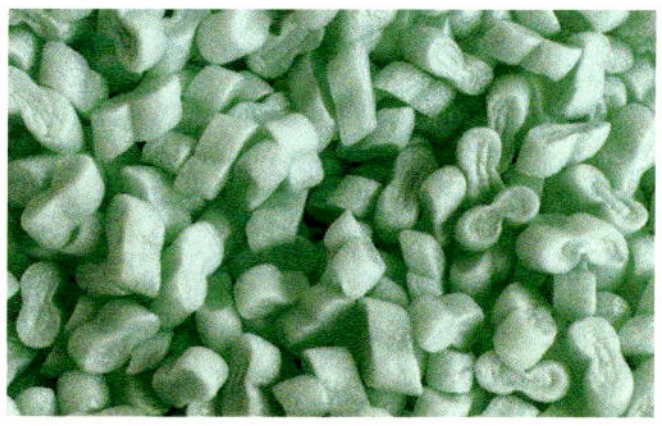
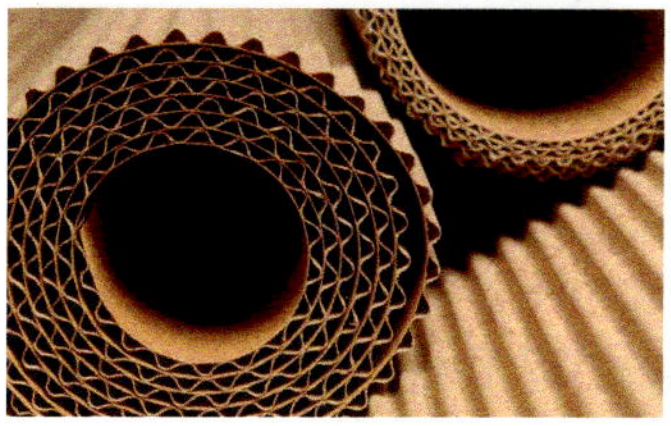

2 Containerisation
Research how the invention of standardised shipping containers contributed to globalisation. Share your results in class.

3 Shipping and handling marks
Match the instructions with the handling marks.

1. sling here
2. centre of gravity
3. use no hooks
4. top
5. fragile, handle with care
6. keep away from heat
7. keep dry
8. flammable
9. radioactive

c Look at the following business transactions and match them with the appropriate Incoterm.

1. Games & Adventure Inc. arranges and pays for the transportation and loading of a consignment of tabletop games on board a cargo plane at San Francisco airport. Games & Adventure Inc. sells 1 San Francisco.
2. Davidson plc is a manufacturer with a very powerful position in the market. As it refuses to bear transportation risks, distributors have to collect goods from the factory. Davidson plc sells 2 .
3. Cumbria Steel plc has agreed to pay the costs of transport by road – including insurance – for a consignment of steel plates from its mill to Magdeburg, the place of delivery named by the buyer. The terms of delivery are 3 .
4. Maschinenbau Brandenburg GmbH imports parts from Taiwan. The Taiwanese manufacturer pays for transportation to the port of Keelung, loading charges, and freight and insurance to Bremerhaven, the port of destination in Germany. Their terms are 4 .
5. Silicon Fen Electronics imports components from Japan. The Japanese manufacturer pays for transportation to Yokohama, the port of shipment, and pays the loading costs. Silicon Fen Electronics has to pay for freight, insurance and all other costs from Yokohama to Cambridge. The Japanese supplier sells 5 .
6. When Palm Top Ltd orders notebooks from India, the Indian manufacturer bears all risks and costs, including UK customs duty, until the notebooks have been delivered to Palm Top's premises in Rawdon, Yorkshire. Their terms are 6 .
7. Ergo Büromöbel regularly supplies office furniture to Svensk Kontor AB, a Swedish wholesaler. The furniture is transported at Ergo Büromöbel's risk and expense by lorry to Svensk Kontor's warehouse in Stockholm, the place of destination named by the buyer. The furniture is then ready to be unloaded from the lorry at Svensk Kontor's convenience. Ergo Büromöbel delivers to Svensk Kontor AB on the terms 7 warehouse in Stockholm.

2 Internet research

Research the following topics and report back in class:

- Deliveries by drones: How will logistics networks change?
- Increasing e-commerce: What changes has it triggered in terms of deliveries? What are the respective advantages and disadvantages?

Dispatch advice and shipping documents

#basic shippingdocs

International trade relies on accurate documentation that meets the regulations of the respective countries. Therefore, the documentation process of international shipping is an essential part of logistics. To ensure that your products get to their destination without any problems, it is important to complete the paperwork properly.

1 Structure of a detailed dispatch advice

a As soon as preparations for the transport of goods are completed, the customer is informed of the impending dispatch. Sometimes the dispatch advice forms part of the order confirmation. Match the different parts of a dispatch advice to the correct numbers.

courteous phrase | packing details | reference to order | transport information | personal salutation | information that the goods are ready for collection or have been dispatched | complimentary close | reference to payment | reference to documents

Subject: Your order No. R7-345 **[1]**

Dear Nicolas, **[2]**

We are pleased to inform you that your cutlery has been shipped today as air freight. **[3]**
It will be transported on Air Quebec flight no. AQ704, which leaves Munich Airport on 3 May at 21:15 and arrives at Montreal Airport at 23:50 local time. **[4]** The cutlery is packed in 1 ULD container. **[5]** A copy of the commercial invoice is attached. **[6]** The required documents (airway bill, commercial invoice, packing list, insurance certificate) accompany the goods. **[7]**

We hope your order will arrive punctually and we look forward to doing business with you again soon. **[8]**

Best wishes, **[9]**

#gram prepositions
#gram relativeclauses

b Study the following dispatch advice and decide which of the alternatives is correct.

Subject: Your purchase (order no. 1870) **1. of / from** 1 May 20.. **2. about / for** 500 jars of Caviar

Dear Mr Angelo,

This is to inform you that your jars are now ready to be dispatched **3. as per / according** this morning's purchase order. Each jar has been wrapped in tissue paper before being packaged into **4. its / it's** own decorative cardboard box. These boxes are packed into heavy-duty containers, 20 to a container, **5. which / who** are then loaded into two wooden cases with ample cushioning material. As requested, the cases **6. had / have been** marked with both the net and gross weights, the order number and your address. The consignment will be delivered CPT Rome, **7. as / like** stated in your order.
Your goods will be put **8. onto / to** flight Alitalia 736 leaving Munich at 10 am on 30 November 20.. and arriving in Rome at 11.30 am. Please find attached a copy of the air waybill and copies of the invoice. We **9. will / would** ask you to pay within 14 days of receipt of the caviar.
We trust that the caviar will reach you in good condition and we look forward to the pleasure of **10. doing / making** business with you again soon.

Yours sincerely,
Dagmar Müller
Head of Exports

#basic shippingdocs

2 Most common shipping documents

a Match the different shipping documents with their German translation.

1 Bill of Lading (B/L)	**A** Packliste
2 Waybill	**B** Handelsrechnung
3 Air Waybill	**C** Zollinhaltserklärung
4 Certificate of Origin	**D** Konnossement
5 Packing List	**E** Frachtbrief
6 Commercial Invoice	**F** Versicherungspolice
7 Insurance Policy	**G** Ursprungszeugnis
8 Customs Declaration	**H** Luftfrachtbrief

b Work with a partner. Do some internet research and come up with a short description for each shipping document.

#skilldelivery

D8 Dispatch

3 Writing a dispatch advice

Sie arbeiten im Bereich Export Logistik im Hauptlager Duisburg von The Bike Factory Europe GmbH (Warehouse and Distribution, Hafenstr. 33 – 39, 47119 Duisburg, warehouse@the-bike-factory…de). Die australische Firma Cycling Sports (125 Kangaroo Road, Melbourne, Victoria 5039/Australien) hatte 200 Mountainbikes der Marke BX 421 zum Einkaufspreis von € 850 bestellt. Gesamtpreis: € 170.000, Lieferbedingung: CIF Melbourne. Heute ist der 12. August 20.. und die Ware ist versendet worden.

Schicken Sie per E-Mail eine Versandanzeige mit heutigem Datum an die australische Firma. Ihre Kontaktperson ist James Head (j.head@cycling_sports…com). Berücksichtigen Sie dabei die folgenden Punkte:

- *200 Fahrräder am 10. August an Bord der YM Unity 12 von Hamburg Hafen abgegangen*
- *Versendung in 10 seefesten Containern*
- *voraussichtliche Ankunft in Melbourne 2. September 20..*
- *Versanddokumente: Originale Konnossement-Nr. TPE07 58233/001 3-fach, Handelsfaktura 3-fach, Originale Ursprungszeugnis 2-fach und eine Kopie, Originale Versicherungspolice 2-fach mit einer Kopie*
- *angemessener Schluss*

! COMMON MISTAKES

1. Transport ~~with~~ **by** lorry …
2. We ~~like~~ **would like** to charter a ship for the transport of …
3. We wish to ~~conclude~~ **take out** insurance for …
4. Please contact the ~~insurance~~ **insurance company**.
5. Please let us know ~~to~~ **on** what terms you can insure a cargo of …
6. The goods will be sent ~~with~~ **by** courier.
7. The lorry left our premises ~~to~~ **for** Paris last night.
8. The consignment will arrive ~~by~~ **at** your warehouse ~~at~~ **on** 14 June.
9. The documents will be released to you ~~from~~ **by** your bank.
10. We hope the goods will arrive ~~punctual~~ **punctually**.

Business scenario

Sie absolvieren ein Praktikum in der Einkaufsabteilung der Baumaschinen KG, einem Hersteller von Baumaschinen in Hamburg. Ihr Unternehmen hat vor fünf Tagen eine Bestellung über Ersatzteile bei der Firma Bramford Ltd. in Newcastle aufgegeben. Die Ersatzteile sind für Ihren Kunden Kuma Mining Germany GmbH bestimmt, der diese Ersatzteile dringend benötigt.

Step 1 A14 Bramford Ltd. hat eine Nachricht in Bezug auf die Bestellung der Ersatzteile auf Ihrer Mailbox hinterlassen. Hören Sie die Nachricht an und fassen Sie den Inhalt für Ihren Vorgesetzten, Stephan Bistram, auf Deutsch zusammen.

Step 2 Eine Stunde später erhalten Sie die folgende E-Mail von Stephan.

> Hallo,
>
> bin gleich in einer Sitzung. Bitte rufe Herrn Kumari an (aus Indien, neu bei Kuma Mining Germany GmbH, spricht kein Deutsch) und erkläre ihm, warum wir die Ersatzteile später bekommen und sich deswegen der Versand seiner Bestellung auch um 2 Tage verzögern wird. Die Verzögerung ist ein Fall von höherer Gewalt.
> Frage ihn bitte bei der Gelegenheit, ob er sich einmal unsere Produktion hier in Hamburg ansehen möchte und welche Termine in Frage kämen.
> Schreibe mir bitte ein kurzes Memo über das Gespräch – gerne auch auf Englisch ☺
>
> Danke
> Stephan

Step 3 Sie rufen Herrn Kumari von Kuma Mining Germany an. Führen Sie das Gespräch mit einem Partner/einer Partnerin. Berücksichtigen Sie die Angaben aus Stephans E-Mail.
→ Role cards, p. 119

Step 4 Schreiben Sie die Gesprächsnotiz für Stephan auf Englisch.

#skillmemo
D3 Memo

Review

Before you test yourself in *Exam practice*, take a few moments to reflect on what you have just learned. Then make a follow-up plan: What do you need to improve before the final exam? How will you go about getting there? You can check again after *Exam practice*.

#basicpacking
#basic incoterms
#basic shippingdocs

In this unit, you have learned …
what you have to consider when sending goods to customers concerning regulations and costs in international trade, packing and labelling, as well as shipping documents | how to use the Incoterms | how to write a dispatch advice

1 Considering these topics and tasks, ask yourself:

#vocabdelivery
#gram prepositions
#gram relativeclauses
#skillmemo
#skilldelivery
#skill phonecall
#vocab phonecall

Vocabulary	Do I know the relevant words and phrases relating to … the different modes of transport | packing and labelling | the Incoterms | the most common shipping documents?
	Can I understand and use these relevant words and phrases confidently in speaking and writing?
	Can I adapt my language to the medium / channel I use (letter, email, phone)?
Grammar	When writing and / or speaking, did I come across a common source of grammar mistakes?
	If so, what was it and how can I practise and improve in this particular area?
Writing	Do I know the structure of a dispatch advice? What do I need to consider when writing a dispatch advice?
	What do I need to consider when writing a memo in German?
	What mistakes are commonly made in correspondence regarding deliveries?
Speaking	Can I make a phone call and inform the customer about a delay in delivery?
Methods / Strategies	Do I know how to spell correctly, and can I take down names and numbers accurately?

2 Use your answers from 1 to create a learning and revision plan:

WHAT? What do I need to work on?	**HOW?** What will I do to improve?	**WHEN?** When do I want to complete this?
…	…	…

TIP

Ways to improve your vocabulary:
- Get into the habit of reading regularly.
- Learn words in context.
- Practise using new words in conversation.

Exam practice

1 Sprachergänzungstest (Bearbeitungszeit ca. 10 Minuten)

Setzen Sie 20 der 23 angegebenen Wörter in die Lücken des Textes ein.

agreed | approximately | bill | box | confirm | consignment | courier | due | duplicate | expected | forwarding | hope | loaded | marking | near | placing | premise | reach | shipping | time | transported | under | watertight

Dear Mr Walter,

Dispatch advice

With reference to yesterday's phone call and your email from 15 September, we are pleased to **1** that the **2** of computer monitors **3** the order no. UK-1301 has now been **4** on board MV Gloria, which is **5** to leave Bremerhaven for the port of Hull in 4 days' **6** .
The articles have been packed in 4 **7** containers with the **8** DE-1301 and will be **9** from Hull to York by our **10** agency, Speedup GmbH. Your order is **11** to arrive at your **12** in **13** seven days.
In the meantime, the **14** documents (clean **15** of lading, commercial invoice and **16** inspection certificates) have been sent to you by post **17** and payment has been received as **18** .
Thank you for **19** your order with our company. We look forward to doing further business with you in the **20** future.

Best regards,
Tony Screen

2 Geschäftsbrief nach Stichworten (Bearbeitungszeit 45 Minuten)

Sie arbeiten im Bereich Export Logistik im Hauptlager Duisburg von The Bike Factory Europe GmbH, Warehouse and Distribution, Hafenstr. 33–39, 47119 Duisburg (warehouse@thebikefactory…de). Die französische Firma Bécanes Sports, 33 Rue Saint-Rémi, 33000 Bordeaux, hatte 120 hochwertige Gravel Bikes, Typ Fastroad bestellt.
Die Ware ist nun versandbereit.
Schicken Sie per E-Mail eine Versandanzeige mit heutigem Datum an die französische Firma. Ihre Kontaktperson ist Louis Marchand (l.marchand@becanessports…com). Berücksichtigen Sie folgende Punkte:

- *Bezugnahme auf obigen Auftrag, Nr. GR 4711*
- *Nicht 20 Kisten mit je 6 Bikes, sondern aus Sicherheitsgründen 24 Kisten mit je 5 Bikes*
- *120 Gravel Bikes gehen Mittwoch per LKW mit der Spedition Globerunner GmbH nach Bordeaux ab*
- *Kisten sind mit Kundenanschrift und Auftragsnummer von Bécanes Sports markiert*
- *Voraussichtliche Ankunft in Bordeaux Ende der Woche*
- *Fahrer wird sich im Lager des Kunden melden*
- *Bitte um kurze Bestätigung der Ankunft der Ware*
- *Bitte um pünktliche Überweisung des Rechnungsbetrages*
- *Angemessener Schluss*

6 STARTER

PAYMENT

#basicpayment

1 Invoice and pro forma invoice

Read the two short definitions and complete the text by filling in the words *invoice* or *pro forma invoice* (also *proforma, pro-forma*).

An [1] is required whenever an individual or a business sells goods or provides services to a client or customer. The [2] is drawn up by the seller and is evidence of the existence of a contract to provide goods or services.

A [3] is not a true [4]. It simply details the commitment of a seller to provide certain goods or services to a buyer and is sent before the actual transaction takes place. In international trade, a [5] may be required for customs or to apply for an import licence in countries where this is required. A [6] contains all the details of the subsequent commercial [7].

2 Elements of an invoice

Which items/elements do you think should be included in an invoice? Discuss in class.

Parts of an invoice and methods of payment

#basic payment

An invoice is a commercial document. It is issued by a seller to a buyer and contains certain information about a sales transaction, like the products, quantities, and prices that have been agreed upon. To settle an invoice, a seller can choose from a range of different means of payment.

#vocab payment
#skillinvoice

1 Sending a pro forma invoice

The Indian wholesaler Patel Office Equipment ordered office chairs from the German manufacturer Ergo Büromöbel GmbH and has asked for a pro forma invoice.
Study this pro forma invoice and say which information is missing. You can find the items that should be included in an invoice in the box.

> date and number of the invoice | name and address of the seller | name and address of the customer or client | date and number of the order | date when the goods or services are provided | exact details of the goods or services | unit price and price for the quantity supplied | details of possible discounts | total amount of invoice | terms of payment and credit period granted | seller's international bank account number (IBAN) and the bank identifier code (BIC) or SWIFT | the seller's VAT registration number where applicable | terms of delivery | mode of transport | net weight and gross weight | details of packaging | transport costs

PRO FORMA INVOICE R-BS31-42/09

ergo
Büromöbel
GmbH

To: Patel Office Equipment
127 Delhi Road
Meerut-250 001
Uttar Pradesh
India

Abt. Vertrieb
An der Iller 44–46
D-87509 Immenstadt
Phone: +49 (0)8323/9552-0...
www.ergobueromoebel...de
Ust. ID No. DE 812 017 779

September 25, 20..

Quantity	Description	Unit price Euro	Total Price Euro
100	Ergonomic Office Chair OFM-241	135.50	13,550.00
100	Ergonomic Task Chair OFM-312	145.20	14,520.00
		Subtotal	28,070.00
		10 % quantity discount	– 2,807.00
		TOTAL CIF Mumbai	**25,263.00**

Please remit the net invoice amount within 30 days from date of commercial invoice to our account with Bayernbank AG, BIC: BABADET T304

2 Different methods of payment

a Brainstorm different methods of payment. Which are used in your company? Share your ideas with a partner.

b Do some research online to get to know more about how the different means of payment work.

c Read the statements below. Match each one with the correct means of payment from the box.

Means of payment

cash | bank transfer | credit card | debit card | cheque | bill of exchange | letter of credit

Definitions

1. Customers use a card with a PIN to enable the money to be transferred to the seller's bank account. The money is taken from the customer's account immediately.
2. The customer arranges a transaction with their bank to have a sum sent from their account to the seller's account.
3. A written slip from the seller to the customer, ordering them to pay the amount immediately or within a given timeframe.
4. A contractual document involving the seller, their bank, the customer and the customer's bank. It is opened by the customer's bank, which at the end also releases the documents required for the goods to be received.
5. A written slip on which the customer promises to pay a sum to the recipient. The recipient takes the slip to their bank and exchanges it for cash or has it paid directly into their account.
6. Money is exchanged immediately at the point of sale, usually in notes and coins.
7. Customers use a card with a PIN to enable the money to be transferred to the seller's bank account. The money is paid by a company which later sends a bill to the customer.

Terms of payment in international trade

#basic payment

The terms of payment chosen in an international transaction will depend on the size of the order, the customer's credit rating, and the banking system and political situation in the customer's country.

1 Terms of payment and risk assessment

a Read the description of the different terms of payment in international trade. Carry out a risk assessment by putting the terms of payment into an order from low to high risk. Start with "cash with order" (low risk) and end with "open account terms" (high risk).

A **Cash with order** (CWO) involves very little risk. The seller demands that payment covering the cost of merchandise and delivery accompany the customer's order.

B **Cash on delivery** (COD) is riskier for the seller. The carrier or postman delivers the goods to the customer and hands them over after the customer has paid the amount in question or the client has shown proof by the bank that the amount has been received.

C In the case of long-term business relationships with trusted relations, or large orders involving the supply of large goods like machinery or services such as the installation of equipment, the seller may also allow **staggered payment**. The payment is spread over a period of time, for example one third with the order, one third on delivery and one third 30 days after delivery.

D **Payment in advance** is similar to CWO. Payment must be effected before shipment. It provides maximum security for the seller, especially when the goods or services are customised.

E Drawing a **bill of exchange** (B/E) is a very risky form of payment but common among customers worldwide. It is used to grant the customer credit for a longer period of time, e.g. 60 days after the bill of exchange has been drawn. When the customer's bank advances the money minus a bank discount long before the bill of exchange is due, the seller receives the money immediately.

F A more complex term is the **documentary letter of credit**. The risk of a delay in payment or default payment is low due to the fact that the customers receive the documents needed to receive the goods only after payment has been made by their bank. A confirmed L/C provides even more security for the exporter as a bank in their own country is responsible for payment.

G The seller can grant the customer credit with **open credit** terms, such as: 30 days net, 10 days 2%. This means that the buyer has to remit the invoice amount within 30 days. If they pay within 10 days, they are entitled to deduct 2% of the invoice amount. These terms provide a high risk for the seller but are widely used in transactions involving small sums or with trusted customers.

H **Payment on receipt of invoice.** The customer has to effect payment on the date when the invoice is received.

I **Open account terms** are typically granted to well-established and trusted business partners. Payment has to be effected after the goods have been delivered. However, the customer does not pay individual invoices but waits for the regular statements of account agreed upon with the seller. These contain the balance outstanding on the customer's account on a fixed date, e.g. the 20th of every month.

b Ergo Büromöbel GmbH offers different terms of payment to different customers. Complete the risk assessment for Ergo Büromöbel GmbH and their customers and suggest suitable terms of payment.

Customers:

1. Office Time Ltd., Edinburgh, reliable customer of office furniture. Ergo Büromöbel is anxious to secure a large order with Office Time Ltd., which insist on being granted credit for 60 days.
2. Le Studio, Brussels, new customer of stationery. They ordered stationery two years ago and had difficulty paying even a small amount of € 50.00.
3. Home-Office Solutions plc, New York, bulk buyer and business partner for two years. They usually buy office equipment worth US $ 50,000.00 every month.
4. Patel Office Equipment, Meerut, new customer from India. They have ordered office furniture worth € 25,263.00.
5. Bankbüros, Zurich, very trusted business partner with regular orders. They have been doing business for 10 years and Bankbüros has never missed payment.
6. New Moon Offices, Tokyo, new customer for customised home office furniture. They have never done business before with Ergo Büromöbel GmbH.

c Work in groups of four and discuss your risk assessments. Give reasons for your choices and present them in class.

#gram prepositions

2 Using the right payment terms

Complete the sentences using the correct term or phrase.

payable at | bill of exchange | on the basis of | as requested | at maturity | in our favour | under our agreement | valid until | for the difference | open account terms | to your account

1. We are enclosing our pro forma invoice ___.
2. We are enclosing our monthly statement of account showing a balance of $ 19,995.05 ___.
3. Enclosed we are sending you our cheque as the first instalment of ___.
4. Please let us have a credit note ___.
5. As we have been doing business ___ documents against payment for five years, we would like to ask you to grant us ___.
6. As arranged, we have drawn on you a ___ at 60 days.
7. Payment is to be effected by irrevocable letter of credit in our favour, ___ a German bank and ___ 30 April.
8. We have transferred the amount ___ with LG bank.
9. We will duly honour the bill ___.

Solving glitches in payment

Agreeing on terms of payment, issuing invoices, and making payments is both an essential as well as sensitive part of doing business. There are many reasons why things can go wrong. In order to maintain good business relations, it is always important to show understanding, communicate politely and know how to clarify the situation.

1 Listening to a voicemail and correcting an invoice

Sakura Sakai from New Moon Offices in Tokyo, a wholesaler for office furniture, left a voicemail for Jochen Hoffmann, head of sales at Ergo Büromöbel GmbH. She refers to a number of discrepancies in the pro forma invoice she received from Ergo Büromöbel GmbH.

A 15 **a** Listen to Ms Sakai's message and look at the pro forma invoice below.

PRO FORMA INVOICE R-TK58-22/06

ergo
Büromöbel
GmbH

To: New Moon Offices
1-6 Nishiikebukuro
Toshima 171-8505
Prefecture Tokyo
Japan

Abt. Vertrieb
An der Iller 44–46
D-87509 Immenstadt
Phone: +49 (0)8323/9552-0...
www.ergobueromoebel...de
Ust. ID No. DE 812 017 779

10 July 20..

Dear Ms Saki,
Thank you for your order for 25 double desks and 25 office chairs.

Quantity	Description	Unit price Euro	Total Price Euro
25	double desk DD-155, atomic grey	257.40	6,435.00
25	office chairs OCC-47	89.80	4,490.00
		Subtotal	10,925.00
		3 % quantity discount	– 327.75
		TOTAL FAS Tokyo	**10,597.25**

Payment is to be made in advance. Shipment will be effected after receipt of payment.

b Now answer Mr Hoffmann's questions in German.

1. Was ist der Grund für Frau Sakais Anruf?
2. Wann benötigt Frau Sakai die Ware?
3. Wie soll die Ware befördert werden?
4. Um welche Zahlungsbedingungen bittet Frau Sakai?

D1 Email D14 Invoice

c Write an email reply to Ms Sakai and include the following details given to you by Mr Hoffmann as well as the corrected pro forma invoice.

- *Danke für Ihre Bestellung NE 155 555 vom 7. Juli*
- *freuen uns mitteilen zu können, dass alle Produkte auf Lager sind*
- *haben bereits Vereinbarungen mit unserem Seehafenspediteur getroffen; können bestätigen, dass die Lieferung Tokio vor dem 30. August erreichen wird*
- *die Bestellung wird CFR Tokio versendet, sobald wir die Benachrichtigung zu Ihrem Dokumentenakkreditiv erhalten haben*
- *anbei korrigierte Proformarechnung*
- *höflicher Schluss und bitte in meinem Namen unterschreiben*

2 Reacting to incorrect payment

Ergo Büromöbel GmbH delivered ergonomic chairs to Patel Office Equipment in India. They received payment which does not cover the whole amount stated on the invoice.

#skillemail **a** Write an email on behalf of Birgit Rasch from the accounts department of Ergo Büromöbel GmbH to Sadhu Patel, Patel Office Equipment, using the details from Ms Rasch's notes below.

- *Bitte schreiben Sie eine E-Mail an Herrn Sadhu Patel, Patel Office Equipment, s.patel@patel-office-equipment...com; Bedanken Sie sich für die Bestellung.*
- *Bestätigen Sie den heutigen Zahlungseingang der Rechnung Nr. R-BS31-42/09.*
- *Machen Sie Herrn Patel höflich darauf aufmerksam, dass der eingegangene Betrag 24.292,00€ beträgt. Die ursprüngliche Rechnungssumme beläuft sich aber auf 25.263,00€. Bitten Sie höflich um eine Rückmeldung, um diese Situation zu berichtigen.*
- *Versenden Sie die E-Mail an Herrn Patel und zur Kenntnis an mich: birgit.rasch@ergobueromoebel...de in Cc; Hängen Sie die Rechnung an die E-Mail an.*

#gramtenses **b** Mr Patel receives the email from Ergo Büromöbel GmbH and checks the online bank remittance form with the invoice. Something went wrong. Mr Patel calls his bank for clarification. He is told that his bank deducted costs for the transaction and the currency exchange, amounting to the equivalent of €971.00, from the amount of the invoice. He realises that he forgot to instruct his bank to debit all the charges to his account.
Mr Patel arranges to have the difference remitted by bank transfer within 36 hours.
Write an email on behalf of Sadhu Patel to Ms Rasch. First apologise for this error and then explain what happened and how you intend to adjust the mistake.

! COMMON MISTAKES

1. … showing a balance of €17.20 ~~to our favour~~ **in our favour**.
2. We have ~~transfered~~ **transferred** the amount ~~on~~ **to** your account ~~by~~ **with** XYZ Bank.
3. Checking your invoice we ~~noted~~ **noticed** the following error.
4. Please ~~notice~~ **note** that part shipments are not allowed.
5. As we ~~are doing business since~~ **have been doing business for** two years …
6. Payment ~~should be made~~ **is to be made** by letter of credit.
7. The bank will open a letter of credit, payable ~~by~~ **at** a German bank and valid ~~up to~~ **until** 31 July.

Business scenario

Als Auszubildende/-r bei der Firma Sorglos GmbH (Schwedenstr. 15, 30161 Hannover), einem Landmaschinenhersteller, haben Sie im Namen Ihres Vorgesetzten Robert Bauer ein Angebot an die schwedische Firma Lantbruk AB (Klockargatan 7, SE-12123 Stockholm, Schweden) geschickt. Sie haben daraufhin, am 5. April, eine Bestellung von Lantbruk AB über 5 Erntemaschinen, Modell EM23, Stückpreis 21.000 Euro erhalten.

Step 1 D14 Invoice

Schreiben Sie im Namen Ihres Vorgesetzten eine Auftragsbestätigung sowie eine Proformarechnung an Ole Sörensen von der Firma Lantbruk AB. Orientieren Sie sich dabei an Ihrem Angebot aus Unit 3 (Seite 32).

Step 2

Wenige Tage nachdem die erste Zahlung von Lantbruk AB eingegangen ist, erhalten Sie einen Anruf von Ole Sörensen. Er erinnert Sie daran, dass beim Besuch in Hannover ein Einführungsrabatt von 5% in Aussicht gestellt wurde. Dieser wurde in der Rechnung nicht berücksichtigt.
Führen Sie das Gespräch mit einem Partner / einer Partnerin. → Role card B, p. 119

Role Card A – Sorglos GmbH

- Nehmen Sie den Anruf der Firma Lantbruk AB freundlich entgegen.
- Sagen Sie, dass Sie die Rechnung auf Ihrem Rechner aufrufen und fragen Sie nach dem Anliegen des Anrufers.
- Sagen Sie, dass Sie sich an diese Vereinbarung erinnern und dass Sie sich dafür entschuldigen, dass der Rabatt nicht ausgewiesen wurde.
- Bieten Sie an, eine Gutschrift über den Rabatt-Betrag für Lantbruk AB auszustellen.
- Bedanken Sie sich für das Verständnis. Kündigen Sie eine E-Mail an, in der Sie das Telefongespräch zusammenfassen werden und stellen Sie in Aussicht, dass die Gutschrift im Lauf der Woche erstellt werden wird.
- Sagen Sie, dass Sie sich über zukünftige Geschäftsbeziehungen freuen und verabschieden Sie sich angemessen.

Step 3

Im Anschluss an Ihr Gespräch mit Herrn Sörensen schreiben Sie eine E-Mail an ihn, um den Inhalt des Gesprächs schriftlich festzuhalten. Sie senden eine Kopie der E-Mail an Ihren Vorgesetzten, Herrn Bauer.

Review

Before you test yourself in *Exam practice*, take a few moments to reflect on what you have just learned. Then make a follow-up plan: What do you need to improve before the final exam? How will you go about getting there? You can check again after *Exam practice*.

#basic payment

In this unit, you have learned how to …
issue a pro forma invoice and a commercial invoice | solve glitches in payment by letter and email | talk about payment in telephone calls | negotiate terms of payment

1 Considering these topics and tasks, ask yourself:

#vocab payment	**Vocabulary**	Do I know all the relevant words and phrases to … talk about terms of payment | talk about means of payment | issue invoices | write emails and letters about discrepancies in payment?
		Can I understand and use these relevant words and phrases confidently in speaking and writing?
		Can I adapt my language to the medium / channel I use (letter, email, phone)?
#gram prepositions #gramtenses	**Grammar**	When writing and / or speaking, did I come across a common source of grammar mistakes? If so, how can I avoid these mistakes and improve in this particular area?
#skillinvoice #skillemail	**Writing**	Do I know the elements an invoice has to contain?
		Do I know the structure of an invoice?
		What do I need to consider when issuing a pro forma invoice?
		What do I need to consider when issuing commercial invoices?
		What do I need to consider when issuing letters or emails to inform business partners about payment / delay in payment / wrong payment?
		What common mistakes are often made when issuing an invoice?
#skill phonecall	**Speaking**	Can I negotiate terms of payment on the phone?
		Can I talk about discrepancies in payment?
	Methods / Strategies	Do I know how to spell correctly and can I take down invoice numbers?

2 Use your answers from 1 to create a learning and revision plan.

WHAT? What do I need to work on?	**HOW?** What will I do to improve?	**WHEN?** When do I want to complete this?
…	…	…

TIP

To improve your speaking skills, listen to native language speakers. There are many tutorials about terms of payment, methods of payment, and issuing invoices on the internet. Try to watch and understand one tutorial per week.

Exam practice

1 Kurzgefasste schriftliche Mitteilung (Bearbeitungszeit 30 Minuten)

Sie arbeiten bei der E-Bike Spezialist GmbH. Einer Lieferung von Aluminium-Rohren für die E-Bike-Rahmen lag eine Rechnung bei, die Unstimmigkeiten aufweist. Herr Nikolai Werner, Ihr Vorgesetzter, legt Ihnen die Rechnung zusammen mit folgendem Vermerk auf den Tisch.

- *bitte diese Rechnung bei Frau Yang beanstanden*
- *Folgende Aspekte stimmen nicht:*
  - *bei Position 1 ist der Betrag falsch, es müssten 2,955.00 US $ sein*
  - *bei Position 2 ist die falsche Menge berechnet worden, die gelieferte Menge ist korrekt, geliefert wurden 115 Stück zum Gesamtpreis von 1.782,50 US $*
- *Bitte um korrigierte Rechnung, da die Zahlung sonst nicht angewiesen werden kann*
- *per E-Mail mit Cc an mich (nikolai.werner@e-bike.spezialist...de)*

Metal Unlimited plc.

E-Bike Spezialist GmbH
Altenhoffmannstr. 222
45128 Essen
Germany

2-6-1 Marunouchi
Chiyoda-ku
Tokyo
Chiyoda-ku, 100-8071

order No. ST22/202-79037
invoice No. IST 12/23-45
31 March 20..

person in charge: Ms Milan Yang
phone: +81 3 6867213-99...
milan.yang@metal...com
www.metal...com

Invoice IST 12/23-45 for aluminium tubes

Thank you for your order of our aluminium tubes, AT169 and AT172.
As agreed, we charge you for the following items:

Pos.	Quantity	Description	Unit Price US$	Total Price US$
1	250	AT169 20.00 mm × 0.5 mm × 1,000.00 mm net kgs 0.86	11.82	2,364.00
2	100	AT172 25.00 mm × 0.7 mm × 1,200.00 mm net kgs 1.61	15.50	1,550.00
			NET TOTAL, CIP Tokyo	**3,914.00**

Please remit the invoice amount within 30 days from the date of invoice to our bank account 1546546133, Bank of Tokyo-Mitsubishi UFJ, BIC: BOTKJPJTXXX. If payment is made within 14 days after the date of invoice, we will grant a 1.5 % cash discount on the total amount of the invoice.

2 Vermerk über einen Geschäftsbrief (Bearbeitungszeit 30 Minuten)

Sie machen eine Ausbildung bei der Ergo Büromöbel GmbH, einem führenden Hersteller und Großhändler für ergonomische Büromöbel. In der Abwesenheit von Herrn Jochen Hoffmann aus der Verkaufsabteilung Asien bearbeiten Sie die eingehende Geschäftskorrespondenz. Heute, am 16. Juni, erhalten Sie ein Schreiben von der Firma New Moon Offices aus Tokio. Fassen Sie den Inhalt des Briefes für Herrn Jochen Hoffmann in einem Vermerk in deutscher Sprache zusammen (vollständige Sätze, keine Übersetzung).

New Moon Offices
1-6-1 Nishiikebukuro
Toshyma 171-85005
Prefecture Tokyo

To: Ergo Büromöbel GmbH
Abt. Vertrieb
An der Iller 44–46
87509 Immenstadt
GERMANY

person in charge: Mr Xian Youn
Phone: +81 9 134453-16...
xian.youn@newmoon-offices...com
www.newmoon-offices...com

order No. TK-43-864/22
pro forma invoice No. PRI15/22-1876
14 August 20..

Your pro-forma invoice PRI15/22-1876 and Letter of credit No SI2022345/LC/14-6-22

Dear Mr Hoffmann,

Thank you for your confirmation pro forma, as referred to above.

We have instructed our bank to issue an irrevocable and confirmed letter of credit in your favour. This is to be confirmed by Barclay's International Bank, Singapore and will expire on 30 September at the latest.

We have also handed over the required documents, which will be sent to your bank in München. Upon presentation of the commercial invoice in quadruplicate, air waybill in triplicate and your certificate of origin in duplicate, your bank will pay out the invoice amount to you.

Please inform us of the exact date of shipment, as the latest date of shipment is 20 September. Partial or transshipments are not allowed.

We trust that the consignment will arrive safely and your products will meet our sustainable quality expectations and our customers' approval.

We look forward to receiving your information on shipment soon.

Yours sincerely,
Xian Youn
Xian Youn
Import Manager

3 Mündliche Prüfung: Telefongespräch (Dauer ca. 20 Minuten)

Üben Sie gemeinsam mit einem Partner / einer Partnerin.
Tauschen Sie nach einem Durchgang die Rollen. → Role card B, p. 120

Role card A – Kandidat/-in

Sie sind Teamassistent/-in bei der Firma SAS Print GmbH, einem führenden Hersteller von bedruckten T-Shirts in Duisburg. Sie haben eine Bestellung der GIVIX LTD, Glasgow, am 7. Februar ausgeführt. Das Rechnungsdatum ist der 10. Februar mit einem Zahlungsziel von 30 Tagen. Heute, am 20. März ist immer noch kein Zahlungseingang zu verzeichnen.
Frau Meyer aus der Buchhaltung hat bereits eine Zahlungserinnerung an den Kunden geschickt.
Die IBAN Ihrer Firma ist DE38 3504 0085 0134 3231 31.
Ihre Vorgesetzte Michaela Kurz bittet Sie Herrn O'Connor von der Firma GIVIX LTD anzurufen, um die Situation zu klären. Sie schreibt Ihnen dazu folgende E-Mail.

Liebe/-r …,

bitte rufen Sie Herrn O'Connor von der Firma GIVIX LTD an, um die ausstehende Rechnung (Nr. R-186-1002/02, Betrag: 2.500,00 Euro) zu klären. Fragen Sie nach, ob mit der Bestellung alles in Ordnung war und ob es ggf. Gründe für die ausstehende Zahlung gibt.

Prüfen Sie zusammen mit ihm, ob Rechnungsbetrag und Kontodaten korrekt sind.

Falls ein Fehler unsererseits vorliegt, bieten Sie Herrn O'Connor an, dass wir einen Nachlass in Höhe von 5% auf den Rechnungsbetrag gewähren.

Besten Dank.
Michaela Kurz

#basiccomplaint COMPLAINTS AND ADJUSTMENTS

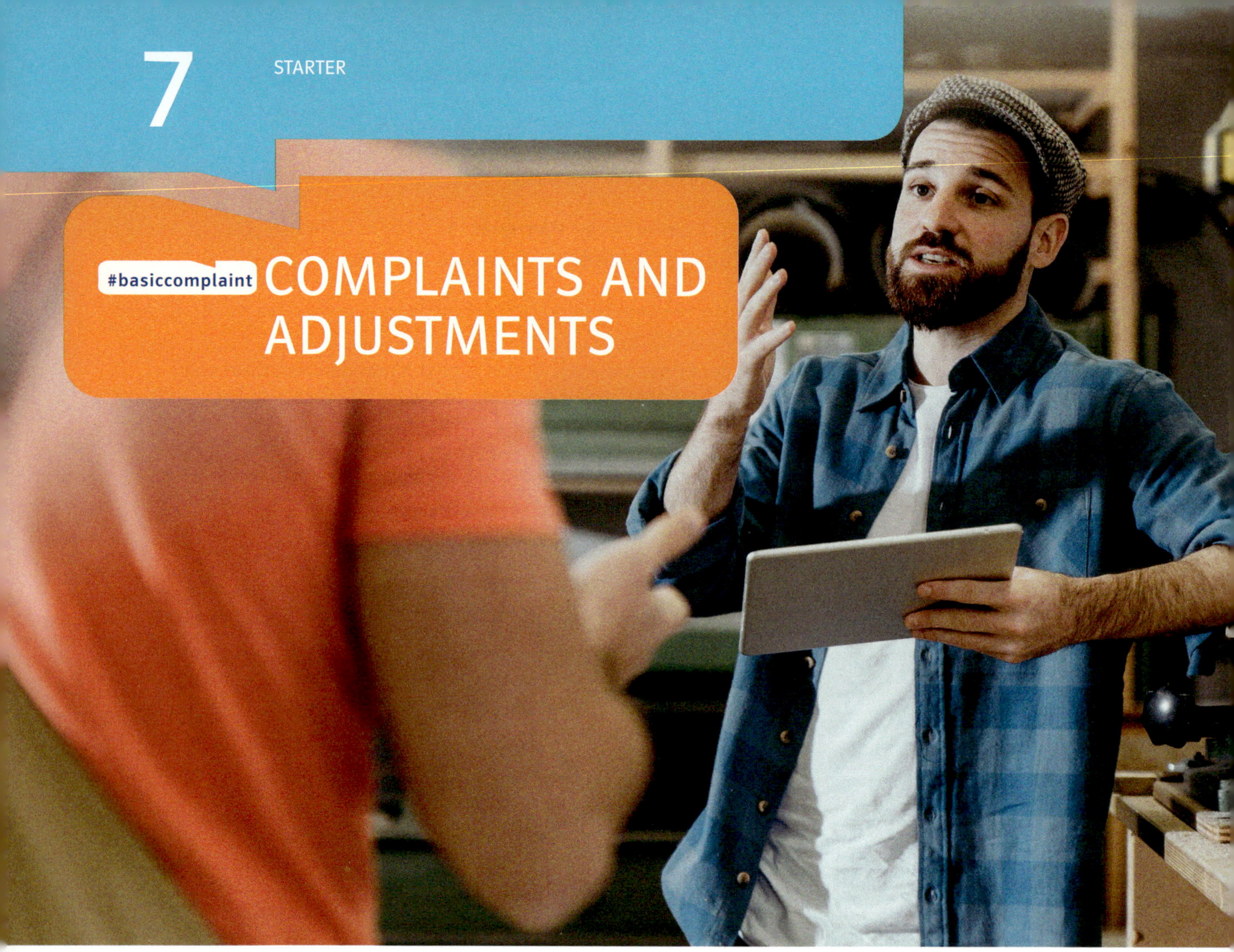

1 Different reasons for complaints

a Think: When did you (or someone you know) have problems with an order? What went wrong? What did you / they do?

b Pair: Talk about your experiences with a partner. Think of possible solutions to your problem.

c Share: Share your results and experiences in class.

2 Essentials of a complaint

What is essential when writing a complaint? Copy the table and complete it with words from the box.

description of the problem | firm | telephone | order number and date | repair | customer's loss or inconvenience | email | invoice number | express delivery | polite | compensation | letter of complaint | discount | date of delivery | unemotional

Ways of communication	Things to be included	Goal of a complaint	Style of language used
…	…	…	…
…	…	…	…

Written complaints

#basic complaint

If there is something wrong with a consignment or transaction, the customer should inform the seller immediately. Often it will be enough just to telephone or send an email in order for the supplier to suggest a solution to the problem. However, if the problem is more serious or the customer feels that his/her complaint is not being taken seriously enough, he/she may decide to write a letter of complaint. Complaints follow certain rules regarding structure and language. Particularly, in the English-speaking world, the language of complaints is far more indirect, polite and conciliatory.

#skill complaint
#vocab complaint

1 Structure of a detailed complaint

Match the parts of a detailed complaint to the corresponding sentences (1–7) in the letter below.

action taken or to be taken by the customer | likely reasons for the problem | salutation | request for prompt adjustment | detailed description of the problem | solution suggested | detailed reference to the order

Dear Mr Jakobeit, [1]

Subject: Our order no. G/L400 for Desk Lamps [2]

Yesterday the consignment of 500 Walnut Wood Adjustable Desk Lamps from the above-mentioned order placed on 10 February was delivered by the forwarder Transcontinental.
On unpacking the boxes, however, our goods inwards inspector found that we had received 600 instead of 500 desk lamps and that the desk lamps are equipped with German Schuco CEE 7/4 plugs and not with British BS 1363 plugs, as required for use in the UK. [3]

We can only assume that our order has been mixed up with another customer's order. [4]

Since we have committed to delivering the majority of the desk lamps we ordered to our own customers by the end of the month, we would ask you to send us the correct number of desk lamps with the right plugs as soon as possible. The goods must reach us by the end of the week, otherwise we shall have no alternative but to cancel the order, however much we may regret such a step. [5]

We are holding the wrong goods at your disposal, pending your instructions. [6]

We trust that you will understand our predicament and do your utmost to have the correct desk lamps dispatched without delay. [7]

Yours sincerely,

Isabella Woodhouse
Isabella Woodhouse
Purchasing Director

2 Being polite

Write down the following direct, rather impolite sentences in a more indirect, polite way.

1. We are dissatisfied with the consignment.
2. We expect you to send replacements immediately.
3. You have made a mistake.
4. If the goods don't arrive on time, we will cancel the order.
5. You must understand our problem.

#skillemail #vocabemail

3 Complaints by email

Chiara Krauss is a trainee in the purchasing department of Wohntraum GmbH. She writes a complaint to Than Chin from Glasses and Jugs Ltd. in China.
Complete her email with 10 of the 12 words below.

with | during | wrongly | until | on | from | despite | damaged | be | find | as soon as | before

From: Chiara Krauss
To: t.chin@glassesandjugsltd...com.cn
Date: 3 November 20..
Subject: Our order No. 6581

Dear Mr Chin,

Thank you for the delivery of the above order. Box No. 1 containing the juice jugs reached us in perfect condition, however we regret to inform you that box No. 2 containing the tumblers was badly **1** and looked as if it had been crushed or dropped **2** transport.
Most of the glasses are broken or chipped and cannot **3** sold. We suggest that you contact your forwarding agent **4** regard to compensation.

5 examination of the enclosed packing list, we found that the wine glasses in box No. 3 differ **6** those we ordered. Our order was for 50 items of article No. GW-3-667. The glasses you supplied seem to be article No. GW-3-668. We would be grateful if you could send us the correct articles **7** possible.

Please **8** enclosed a detailed list of the damaged goods. These will be stored at our warehouse **9** we hear from you. We will also keep the box with the **10** delivered wine glasses so that your hauliers can return them to you when they deliver the correct articles.

Best regards,
Chiara Krauss
Purchasing Department

#vocab complaint
#skillmemo
D3 Memo

4 Receiving a complaint by email

Sie arbeiten für die Firma Solarspeicher AG in Rostock. Sie haben eine Beschwerde von Alba Gomez von der Firma Nova Solar (Málaga, Spanien) erhalten. Lesen Sie die Beschwerde und erstellen Sie einen Vermerk auf Deutsch für Ihren Chef, Mark Fuchs.

From: alba.gomez@novasolar…es
To: m.fuchs@solarspeicher…de
Date: 28 November 20..
Subject: Late delivery of Solar 5 batteries in black battery boxes

Dear Mr Fuchs,

We refer to our order SB 345 dated 23 October for 400 Solar 5 batteries in white battery boxes and 300 Solar 5 batteries in black battery boxes, which you said you could deliver ex stock.
We received the 400 Solar 5 batteries in white battery boxes on time, however, the 300 Solar 5 batteries in black battery boxes are now two weeks overdue.
Over the phone on 22 November, you promised delivery within four days.
As we need the batteries urgently, we will be forced to cancel this order unless we receive the batteries within the next week. We expect you to bear the charges for express delivery.

Yours sincerely,
Alba Gomez
Purchasing Manager

#skill complaint
#vocab complaint
D7 Complaint

5 Writing a letter of complaint

Sie haben eine Ausbildung als Industriekaufmann/-frau mit der Zusatzqualifikation Englisch abgeschlossen und arbeiten für das süddeutsche Unternehmen Motorenwerke Böblingen (Stuttgarter Straße 20, 07031 Böblingen). Ihr Chef, Mark Eggensperger, hat Sie gebeten, in seinem Namen einen Beschwerdebrief an Frau Heywood von AB Filter Technology Ltd. (121 Alton Road, Guildford, GU 34 9LZ) wegen der letzten Lieferungen und der Bestellung Nr. PFP-426 vom 4. September zu schreiben. Folgende Punkte müssen in Ihrem Brief enthalten sein:

- *regelmäßige Bestellung von Filtern und Filterkartuschen seit vier Jahren*
- *drei Jahre lang sehr zufrieden*
- *seit einem Jahr lassen Leistung und Qualität nach und wurden immer schlechter (Ware nicht auf Lager, immer längere Lieferzeiten, tagelang keine Antwort auf E-Mails, immer andere Personen am Telefon)*
- *allein in diesem Jahr wurden einmal der falsche Filter und einmal zu wenig Kartuschen geliefert*
- *aktueller Vorfall heute: Zusendung von fünf Kartuschen des Typs HPC 171b statt wie bestellt HPC 161b*
- *Bitte um unverzügliche Zusendung der richtigen Kartuschen und Abholung der falschen Kartuschen durch den Lieferanten*
- *Drohung den Liefervertrag nicht zu verlängern, sollte keine Besserung in den nächsten drei Monaten eintreten*
- *Hoffnung, dass so ein Schritt nicht notwendig sein wird*
- *Angemessener Schluss*

Adjusting complaints in writing

If a customer complains about a consignment or service, you should always take it seriously, however minor, and deal with it promptly. You should always respond in a positive way and convey to the customer that you appreciate and regret the inconvenience caused. If you decide that the complaint is justified, you will either grant the adjustment as suggested by the client or suggest a possible compromise which must take the customer's interests sufficiently into account. If the complaint is unjustified, explain your reasoning before rejecting it.

1 Structure of a detailed adjustment letter

Match the different parts of a detailed adjustment letter to the corresponding sentences (1–9) in the letter below.

suggestions for adjustment | goodwill ending | action to be taken by customer | reference to complaint | subject line | promise of improvement | investigation/explanation | apologies | salutation

Dear Ms Woodhouse, [1]

Subject: Your order no. G/L400 for 500 Walnut Wood Adjustable Desk Lamps [2]

We have just received your complaint regarding your above-mentioned order, informing us of a most regrettable mix-up of orders. [3]
Please accept our apologies for the inconvenience caused by this mistake on our part. [4]

You were quite right. Your order was indeed mixed up with an Austrian customer's order. I investigated the matter immediately and found out that the mix-up was caused by a person hired from a temporary work agency during the Easter holiday season. [5]

500 Walnut Wood Adjustable Desk Lamps with BS1363 plugs will be dispatched to you free of charge by lorry first thing tomorrow morning. The forwarder, Transcontinental, have given us the assurance that the consignment will arrive at your distribution centre in Basingstoke by Wednesday afternoon at the latest.
To make up for the inconvenience caused, we will grant you a 5 % discount on your next order. [6]
Please hand over the consignment sent by mistake to the Transcontinental driver, who will issue a formal receipt. [7]

We will assure you that we will take all possible steps to ensure that such a mistake will not occur again [8] and hope that this unfortunate incident will not affect our excellent business relationship. [9]

Yours sincerely,
Jens Jakobeit
Jens Jakobeit
Sales Manager

D10 Complaint response

2 Adjustments by email

Mr Than Chin, Sales Manager from Glasses and Jugs Ltd. answers Chiara's email. Read the email and choose the correct alternative.

From: Glasses and Jugs
To: Chiara Krauss
Date: 4 November 20..
Subject: Re: Our order No. 6581

Dear Ms Krauss,

Thank you for your email **1. of / from** this morning. I was extremely sorry to hear that the above order had not been delivered to your full satisfaction and I wish to **2. excuse me / apologise** for the inconvenience caused by this mistake on our part.

I have looked into this matter and it seems that the **3. damage is / damages are** due to rough handling and that the problem lies **4. by / with** the shipping department. We will monitor the department's performance more carefully in the future.
The damaged glasses will of course be exchanged **5. with / through / for** new ones.

As you mentioned in your email, box No. 3 contained 50 items of article No. GW-3-668 instead of 50 items of article No. GW-3-667. The error occurred due to the fact that the packages are **6. practically / practical** identical.
The correct glasses have already been arranged for **7. immediate / immediately** dispatch and will be sent to you at our **8. expenditure / expense** .

You may return the wrongly delivered goods **9. to / at** our risk and expense or hand them over to our hauliers when they deliver the correct articles.

We have maintained an excellent business relationship **10. since / for** many years and I hope this will continue.
I look forward to **11. doing / do** business with you again in the future.

Best wishes,
Than Chin
Sales Manager

3 Types of adjustment

Match each type of adjustment to the correct definition.

discount | express delivery | replacement | substitute | repair | release from contract

1. the fastest way of dispatching goods
2. a new delivery of identical goods
3. granting a reduction of the usual price
4. terminating a supplier relationship (due to their inadequate performance)
5. the act of restoring something damaged or faulty to a good condition
6. a new delivery of similar products

Making and adjusting complaints over the phone

If you are dissatisfied with a consignment, the quickest way to solve the problem is over the phone because you can make both the complaint and adjustment at the same time. If you know the person you are ringing, you usually ask how they are doing before you get down to business. If you are about to mention a problem, you should be firm but polite so that the issue can be solved to the satisfaction of all parties concerned.

A 16 ◁)) **1 Calling Moreale Cosmetics**

Jasmin Kulzer from Kufstadt GmbH calls Chris Peters from Moreale Cosmetics. Listen to the dialogue and complete the transcript with the missing words.

Chris Peters: Good morning. Moreale Cosmetics Inc., Chris Peters on the [1]. How can I help you?

Jasmin Kulzer: Hello Chris, this is Jasmin from Kufstadt GmbH in Augsburg. How are you [2]?

Chris Peters: Nice to hear from you. I'm doing great. [3] about you Jasmin, how are you?

Jasmin Kulzer: I'm fine too. [4] busy at work, though. I'm calling about our [5] for 10 cases of Moreale TechOne and 10 cases of TechTwo hair gel which we [6] at the end of November. The [7] was KS-674.

Chris Peters: Let me just check that on my computer. OK, I've found it. Did something go [8]?

Jasmin Kulzer: [9] something did go wrong. When we unpacked the goods, we [10] that two cases of the Moreale TechOne gel were missing.

Chris Peters: I'm sorry to hear that. I really have to [11] for that mistake. I'll send out the missing cases [12].

Jasmin Kulzer: That would be perfect, as we need them [13]. Thanks a lot.

Chris Peters: You're [14]. I hope to hear from you again soon. Goodbye.

Jasmin Kulzer: Goodbye and thanks a lot for your help.

2 How to deal with complaints over the phone

A 17 ◁)) **a** Copy the following table. Then listen to the three dialogues and complete the table.

Dialogue	Problem	Action taken	Reason for problem	Adjustment
1	...	...	...	...
2	...	...	...	...
3	...	...	...	...

b Discuss the following points in class.

1. Was the complaint properly dealt with?
2. How would you have acted in these situations?
3. Have you experienced any similar situations?

3 Role play: Making a complaint about wrongly delivered goods

#skill phonecall
#vocab phonecall

Ruth Bennet, Purchasing Manager at The Bike Factory in Leipzig placed an order with Guptha Rubbers PLC in Mumbai for heavy-duty tyres. When the consignment arrives in Leipzig, Ms Bennet learns that the tyres which have been sent are the wrong size. She calls Rahul Khan, Sales Manager at Guptha Rubbers, to inform him and to discuss a possible adjustment. Work with a partner. Take the roles of Ruth Bennet and Rahul Khan. Look at the prompts below and act out the telephone conversation.

Rahul Khan	Ruth Bennet
Guptha Rubbers, Rahul Khan speaking / how help?	
	hello / Ruth Bennet, The Bike Factory Europe / reason for calling: order for heavy-duty tyres
hope everything alright	
	afraid / something wrong with last consignment
sorry to hear / order number?	
	IN 234-324
which goods ordered? / what is wrong?	
	500 sets of Badger X3 heavy-duty tyres / diameter of 26 inches / received 250 sets in the wrong size, 28 inches
very sorry / mix-up / just found your order / ordered 26-inch tyres only / what do? / keep tyres? / 5 % discount on the invoice amount?	
	5 % not enough / do not need so many tyres of bigger size / store them for quite a while / extra costs / 20 % discount?
20 % not possible / might be able to offer a 12 % discount / but first check with my boss	
	sounds okay / when expect missing 250 sets of 26-inch tyres? / need them in three weeks' time
no problem at all / get back to you later today / my boss's decision	
	perfect / expect your call as soon as possible / goodbye

! COMMON MISTAKES

1. I refer to our order ~~about~~ **for** heavy-duty tyres.
2. One article is ~~complete~~ **completely** damaged.
3. The ~~damages are~~ **damage is** due to …
4. We wish to ~~excuse us~~ **apologise** for …
5. Please replace the faulty goods ~~by~~ **with** new ones ~~to~~ **at** your expense.
6. We will keep the goods ~~to~~ **at** your disposal.
7. The problem lies ~~by~~ **with** the shipping department.
8. The faulty articles will be exchanged ~~with / through~~ **for** working ones.
9. We would suggest ~~to refer~~ **referring / that we refer** the matter to arbitration.

Business scenario

Sie arbeiten im Kundenservice von The Bike Factory Europe in Leipzig. Vor drei Tagen haben Sie eine Lieferung von 100 Fahrrad T-Shirts an Cycling Ltd. in Belfast geschickt. Ihr Vorgesetzter Richard Becker hat heute eine E-Mail von Cycling Ltd. bekommen.

Step 1 Fassen Sie die wichtigsten Inhalte der Nachricht für Ihren Vorgesetzten in ganzen Sätzen auf Deutsch zusammen.

From: nancy.mcmara@cyclinglimited…ie
To: richard.becker@thebikefactory…de
Subject: Our order No. DE 32465/2B

Dear Mr Becker,

We received your shipment of our order for 100 "Hurricane" cycling T-shirts today.
We regret to inform you that we have been sent the wrong order. On opening the boxes we immediately saw that the T-shirts we had been sent were not only the wrong colour but also only one size, L. We originally ordered 25 shirts of each of the sizes S, M, L and XL, and we selected the dark blue colour, while the T-shirts we received were black.

We are however willing to keep 30 of the T-shirts at a reduced price.
Since we will need the dark blue shirts for a cycling event on next week's Bank Holiday Monday, we expect a replacement delivery by the end of this week. The consignment should consist of 25 dark blue T-shirts in each of the sizes S, M, L and XL.

I would be grateful if you could get back to me with suggestions on how to settle the matter and what we should do with the other 70 black shirts.

Best wishes,
Nancy McMara
Sales Manager

Step 2 Nachdem Sie für Herrn Becker die Nachricht auf Deutsch zusammengefasst haben, schreibt er Ihnen folgende E-Mail. Arbeiten Sie zu zweit und führen Sie das Telefonat. Tauschen Sie anschließend die Rollen. → Role card B, p. 120

Liebe/-r …,
ich bin gerade in einem wichtigen Meeting und kann Nancy McMara nicht selbst anrufen.
Teilen Sie ihr bitte mit, dass der Fehler auf unserer Seite liegt und entschuldigen Sie sich. Es gab eine Verwechslung mit den Bestellungen. Sagen Sie ihr, dass wir die Ersatzlieferung noch heute per Express abschicken. Bieten Sie ihr ebenfalls an, dass sie die falsch gelieferten T-Shirts mit einem Rabatt in Höhe von 10 % behalten kann. Die restlichen 70 T-Shirts kann sie dem Spediteur wieder mitgeben.
Bitte schreiben Sie mir eine kurze Telefonnotiz und informieren Sie mich über das Ergebnis des Telefonates.
Vielen Dank.
Richard Becker

Step 3 Fassen Sie die Ergebnisse des Telefongespräches mit Nancy McMara für Ihren Vorgesetzten auf Deutsch zusammen.

Review

Before you test yourself in *Exam practice*, take a few moments to reflect on what you have just learned. Then make a follow-up plan: What do you need to improve before the final exam? How will you go about getting there? You can check again after *Exam practice*.

#basic complaint

In this unit, you have learned how to . . .
write complaints and adjustments by email and letter | make complaints and adjustments over the phone | give reasons for a complaint | describe a problem with a consignment | give likely reasons for a problem | suggest solutions | apologise | offer different types of adjustments | promise improvement | write a memo in German about a complaint

1 Considering these topics and tasks, ask yourself:

#vocab complaint

#skill complaint

#skill phonecall

Vocabulary	Do I know the relevant words and phrases needed to . . . write complaints and adjustments by letter or email | make a complaint and adjustment on the phone | give reasons for a complaint | describe a problem with a consignment | give likely reasons for a problem | suggest solutions | apologise | offer different types of adjustments | promise improvement?
	Can I understand and use these relevant words and phrases confidently in speaking and in writing?
	Can I adapt my language to the medium / channel I use (letter, email, phone)?
Grammar	When writing and / or speaking, did I come across a common source of grammar mistakes? If so, what was it and how can I practise and improve in this particular area?
Writing	Do I know how to structure a complaint?
	Do I know how to structure an adjustment?
	What do I need to consider when writing a memo about a complaint in German?
	What common mistakes are often made when writing complaints and adjustments?
Speaking	Can I make a complaint/adjustment over the phone?
Methods / Strategies	Do I know how to talk over the phone to business partners I know personally?
	Do I know how to be firm and polite when mentioning a problem?

2 Use your answers from 1 to create a learning and revision plan:

WHAT? What do I need to work on?	**HOW?** What will I do to improve?	**WHEN?** When do I want to complete this?
...	...	...

TIP

Using apps to practise words and phrases can help you to improve your English.
You can practise by playing games or making quizzes and you usually get instant feedback.
Try to make a habit of practising words and phrases at least twice a week.

Exam practice

1 Geschäftsbrief nach Stichworten (Bearbeitungszeit 45 Minuten)

Sie sind Auszubildende/-r bei der Firma Orient Express GmbH, Oldenburger Str. 91, 27753 Delmenhorst. Ihre Firma hatte von einem neuen Lieferanten, dem malaysischen Hersteller von traditionellen Textilien Golden Sun bhd, Level 24, Block C, Platinum Sentral, 50470 Kuala Lumpur, Hals- und Schultertücher bestellt. Die Sendung ist gestern angekommen, entspricht aber nicht ganz den Erwartungen.

Ihr Chef, der Einkaufsleiter Wolfgang Elmer, bittet Sie, einen Brief in englischer Sprache an Golden Sun bhd zu formulieren, den er unterschreiben wird. Folgende Punkte sollen Sie berücksichtigen:

- *Ansprechpartnerin: Ms Marina Ratnasari*
- *Datum: 13. September 20..*
- *Ihr Auftrag vom 02. August 20.., Ihre Auftragsnummer: MY-87-13*
- *Ware pünktlich eingetroffen*
- *leider folgende Beanstandungen:*
  - *50 der bestellten 150 Seidenhalstücher, Best. Nr. 769, fehlen.*
  - *10 der bestellten 100 Schultertücher, Best. Nr. 681, sind stark verfärbt und daher unverkäuflich.*
  - *Die 50 bestellten Schultertücher, Best. Nr. 687, entsprechen farblich und was das Muster angeht nicht der Katalogbeschreibung.*
- *Ihr Vorschlag zur Regelung:*
  - *Sofortige Nachlieferung der fehlenden 50 Seidenhalstücher, für die große Nachfrage besteht.*
  - *Sie sind bereit, die 50 Schultertücher mit der Best. Nr. 687 zu behalten, wenn Ihnen ein Preisnachlass gewährt wird.*
  - *Sie bitten um Mitteilung, was mit den verfärbten Schultertüchern geschehen soll.*
- *Bitte um Stellungnahme und umgehende Bearbeitung Ihrer Reklamation*

Bitte verfassen Sie einen vollständigen Brief mit Absenderadresse, Anschrift, Datum, Anrede, Betreff, Grußformel, Namen der Firma, Namen und Position des Unterzeichners und evtl. Anlagevermerk, der in der äußeren Form britischen bzw. amerikanischen Gepflogenheiten entspricht.

A18 2 Vermerk über ein Telefongespräch (Bearbeitungszeit 20 Minuten)

In dem folgenden Gespräch sind Sie Marcus Friedel von der Firma Büromöbel Bremer in Erfurt. Heute ist der 7. Juni. Sie erhalten einen Anruf von einem Kunden in Großbritannien. Verfolgen Sie das Gespräch und fertigen Sie anschließend für Ihre Geschäftsführerin, Angela Rentmeister, eine entsprechende Gesprächsnotiz auf Deutsch an.

Marcus Friedel	T. Scott
Büromöbel Bremer, Friedel, Guten Tag.	...
I'm afraid he's on a business trip in Turkey so I'm standing in for him at the moment. Can I be of any assistance?	...
Could you give me the order number please? I'll bring it up on my computer.	...
Yes, here it is. I see it wasn't delivered on time but was a few days late. I'm very sorry about that – I hope it hasn't caused you any inconvenience.	...
Oh. I'm very sorry to hear that.	...
I'm sorry about that. I'll just make a note of this. So, altogether three desk packs and three chairs are defective. We'll send you replacements as soon as possible. Was there anything else?	...
I really am very sorry that we have caused you this inconvenience. At the moment I have no idea how it could have happened.	...
I can appreciate that and I can assure you that you are a very important customer as far as we are concerned. I will let our export manager know as soon as he returns. In the meantime, I'll check with my boss as to what we can do to remedy the situation and I'll get back to you by email in the next couple of hours. Again, I very much regret what has happened.	...
Definitely!	...

Büromöbel Bremer

Gesprächsnotiz

Für: ...

Verfasst von: ... am: ...

Gesprächspartner/-in: ...

Betreff: ...

...

#basicreminder REMINDERS

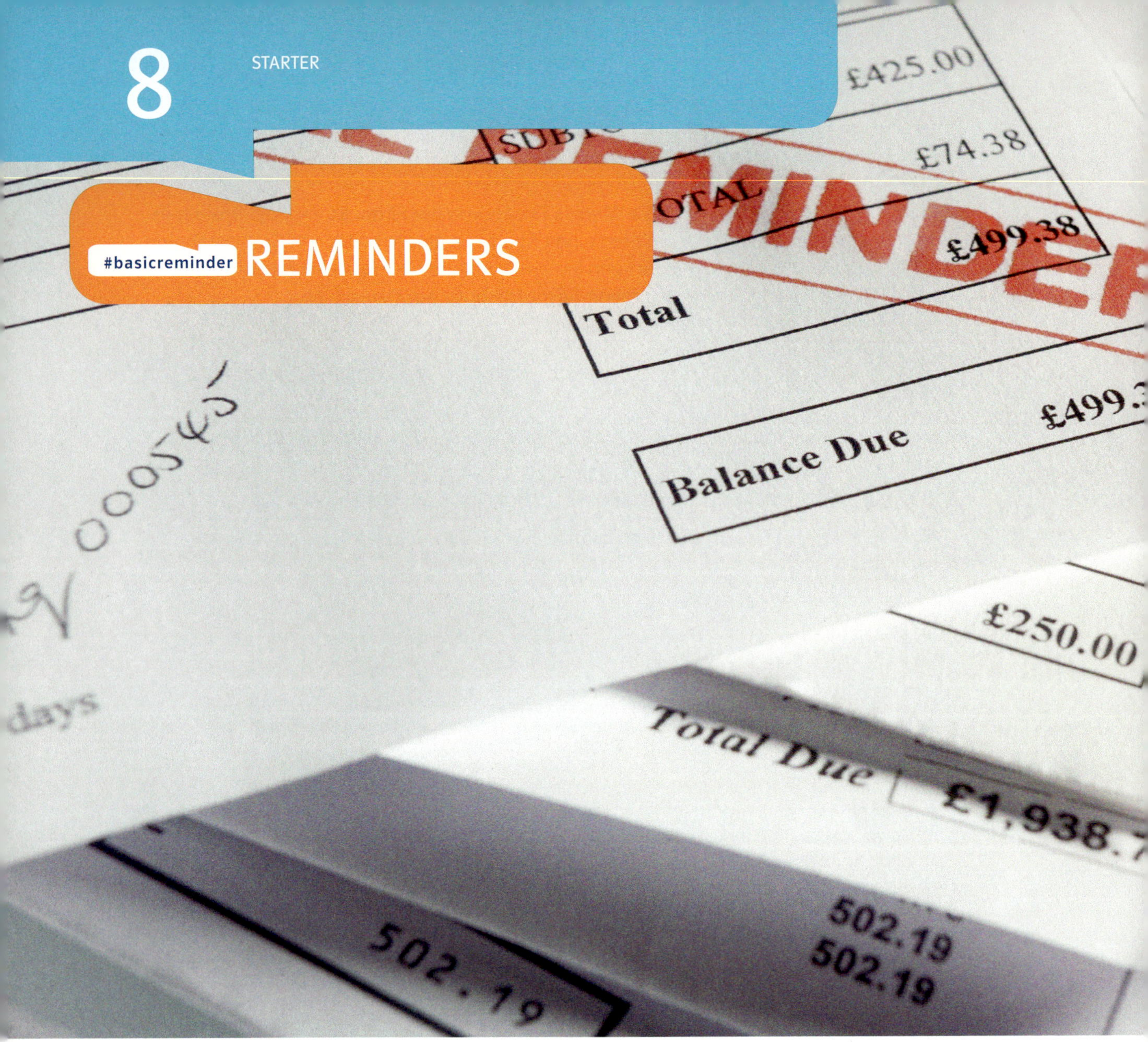

1 Discuss the following questions with a partner and share your results in class.

1. What reasons might a customer have for not paying an invoice?
2. What is a good way of protecting yourself against bad debts (*Forderungsausfälle*)?
3. What should you do before sending goods to a customer?
4. What can suppliers do to encourage prompt payment?
5. What do you think about borrowing money? (advantages/disadvantages)

2 Essential parts of a reminder

What do you think is essential for a reminder? What contents should be included, and what is important when it comes to style and tone? Discuss in class and make a list.

Requesting payment

#basic reminder

Business transactions are increasingly based on the granting credit and it is quite normal that outstanding invoices are not always settled on time. There is probably no company whose accounts department has not spent a large amount of time trying to get customers to pay outstanding invoices.

#vocab reminder

1 Structure of a detailed reminder

a Match the different parts of a detailed reminder to the corresponding sentences (1–8) in the letter below.

suggestion of oversight on debtor's part | salutation | request for payment, setting a deadline | steps to be taken unless payment is made | reference to statement of account/due date/ previous reminder | complimentary close | request explanation, if appropriate | goodwill ending

> Dear Ms Pratt, [1]
>
> We refer to our email of 30 October asking for settlement of our statement of account No. UK/140-77 of 30 September, which is now five weeks overdue. [2]
>
> Unfortunately, it seems that you have overseen the statement of account. [3] As you have always paid your bills promptly, we are at a loss to understand this delay in payment. [4]
>
> Nevertheless, we must ask you to remit the invoice amount within the next 10 days. [5] Should you fail to settle the account within this period, we will unfortunately have to reconsider the terms of payment. [6]
>
> We trust, however, that you will remit the outstanding amount in the next few days and that our cordial business relations can be continued. [7]
>
> Yours sincerely, [8]
>
> ...

b What is the purpose of the following sentences? Match the sentences (A–G) with the appropriate parts of a detailed reminder from exercise a.

A We wish to point out that your account still shows an outstanding balance of $7,234.50 in our favour.

B You have not yet replied to our reminder from 3 June. Should you have any particular reason for withholding payment, please let us know immediately.

C Your arrears in payment constitute a breach of contract. We are considering breaking off business relations with you.

D We would, therefore, ask you to remit the outstanding amount by the end of the week.

E We hope that this matter will soon be settled to the satisfaction of both parties.

F As we have now been waiting for settlement of our invoices for three months, we regret that we will have to institute legal proceedings against you unless the balance of £745.90 is remitted to our account by 31 July.

G Since you have always been a reliable customer, we assume that this invoice must have been overlooked.

2 Features of reminders

It is often necessary to send several written reminders to achieve the desired result. They will gradually become more insistent in tone, the seller being mindful of the customer's payment record. The interval between the reminders may vary.
Read the details below and say if they describe a first, second or final reminder.

1. The first written reminder …	2. The second reminder …	3. The final reminder …

A … may often be included in other correspondence (hidden reminder).
B … will be more insistent.
C … could be used by the supplier to suggest reconsidering terms of payment if the invoice remains unpaid, but he / she should still emphasise that he/she wishes to continue business relations.
D … will point out that the customer will also have to pay interest on arrears.
E … includes a copy of the invoice or statement of account.
F … sets a final deadline for payment.
G … will appeal to the customer's sense of fairness and his desire to maintain his reputation by stressing the consequences of non-payment.
H … should be positive, understanding and avoid blaming the customer.
I … should still be friendly, asking for an explanation but perhaps offering help while requesting payment.
J … warns the customer that should he / she fail to meet the deadline, the matter will be handed over to a collection agency or a solicitor, while at the same time expressing regret at having to take this step.

#skill reminder
#skillemail

3 First reminder

Study this statement of account recording invoices for three deliveries from AB Filter Technology to Motorenwerke Böblingen and a credit note for a sum that had to be paid by AB Filter Technology to Motorenwerke. Then read the lines on page 87. Find the correct sentences and put them in the right order for the email the statement was attached to.

AB Filter Technology

AB Filter Technology Ltd
121 Alton Road • Guildford • GU34 9LZ
Tel. 01962 843690... • Fax 01962 8436911...
www.ab-filtertechnology-uk...com

V.A.T. reg. no. GB234 933351

Statement as per 30 Sept 20..

Motorenwerke Boeblingen
Stuttgarter Str. 20
07031 Boeblingen
Germany

DATE	INVOICE	DEBIT	CREDIT	BALANCE
BALANCE FORWARDED 01-Sept-20..				33,705.00
05-Sept-20..	7045/09/Ger	1,802.00		35,507.00
17-Sept-20..	7069/09/Ger	9,210.00		44,717.00
20-Sept-20..			344.00	44,373.00
27-Sept-20..	7082/09/Ger	3,782.00		48,155.00

A Please transfer the amount due to your account.
B Yours sincerely,
Richard Blake
C We are enclosing our statement of your account for September, which shows a balance of £48,155.00 in our favour.
D Dear Mrs Hasenfuss,
E We are enclosing our statement of your account for September, which shows a balance of £33,705.00 in your favour.
F Please transfer the amount due to our account.
G Yours faithfully,
Richard Blake

#gramtenses
#grammodals

4 Second reminder

Yay! Event Management GmbH is an event management company with its headquarters in Düsseldorf. The company has recently organised a promotional campaign for its long-standing customer, Amperlite Ltd., 24 Harold's Cross, Dublin 6W, Ireland. Since a previous reminder has not been answered by the client, Yay! sends this letter.
Read the letter and choose the correct alternative.

4 November 20..

Dear Mr Darty,

Our invoice no. AL/2021-07 dated 2 September 20..

We 1 to our first reminder dated 25 October 20.. and once again enclose a copy of our statement 2 an overdue balance for the amount of € 1,245.
This amount 3 overdue for more than two months now and we 4 understand why you 5 to settle the balance so far.
We 6 doing business with you for many years and 7 very sorry to lose you as our customer.
However, we 8 no choice but to ask you to arrange the settlement of the outstanding balance by 14 November 20.. at the very latest.

Kind regards,
Michael Strote
Key Account Manager
Yay! Event Management GmbH

1. refer, do refer, referred
2. showed, showing, had shown
3. is, was, has been
4. cannot, could not, have not
5. failed, fail, have failed
6. enjoy, have enjoyed, are enjoying
7. are, would be, have been
8. have, had, are having

#vocab reminder

5 Final reminder

When the deadline passes without payment or a letter from the client, Yay! sends this final reminder. Complete the letter, using the words from the box.

balance | reference | interest | relationship | reminders | legal | amicable

16 November 20..

Dear Mr Darty,

Our invoice no. AL/2021-07 dated 2 September 20..

With 1 to our above-mentioned invoice and two 2 sent to you in October and November respectively, we regret having to inform you that the outstanding amount of € 1,245 is still overdue.
I have repeatedly offered you the chance to communicate with me and find an 3 solution to the matter. However, we have received neither payment nor communication from your end.
In view of our long-standing business 4 , we are herewith granting you a further 10 days in which to settle the outstanding 5 .
Should the invoice not be settled by then, we have no choice but to take 6 action to enforce payment. Please be informed that, in this event, you will also be charged with 7 and legal fees.

I very much hope that litigation will not be necessary.

Yours sincerely,
Michael Strote
Key Account Manager
Yay! Event Management GmbH

A 19 #skill reminder

6 Writing a first reminder

Listen to the conversation between Janice Humble and Jeremy Atkins in the accounts department at Garden of Eden. Draft a letter to Gärtnerei Strobel to remind them that payment is now overdue. Below is a copy of the relevant invoice.

INVOICE NO. GS 13-89 — Customer Ref. GSD78

Mr Heribert Strobel
Gärtnerei Strobel
Am Schlosspark 2
07330 Probstzella
Germany

Date: 4 March 20..
Your Order No. 255 of 5 Feb 20..
POC: Jeremy Atkins
Email: accounts@gardenofeden...co.uk
Tel: 0044 1534 800 776...

QTY	Description	Unit Price	Total
20	Acer japonicum	£ 45.00	£ 900.00
10	Catalpa bigonioides	£ 35.00	£ 350.00
		TOTAL PRICE	£ 1,250.00

#skill reminder
#vocab reminder

D11 Reminder

7 Writing a reminder

Study the invoice and your boss's notes and write an email to Ms Elaine Greenway at elaine@finedine…co.uk. Your boss is the export manager Georg Roth.

INVOICE TO

Finedine Ltd.
26 Madeira Drive
Brighton
BN2 8LT
United Kingdom

INVOICE GBFD 2827

Comestas-Gourmet GmbH
Albert-Schweitzer-Allee 127
22044 Hamburg
Germany
Tel. (0049) 40 275 3766…
customerservice@comestasgourmet…de

USt.ID No. DE 233 909 621

DELIVERY ADDRESS (if different from inv. addr.)

DATE OF INVOICE	YOUR ORDER NO:	DATE OF SUPPLY	TYPE OF SUPPLY
28 Mar 20..	HK 45/12	20 March 20..	
QUANTITY	DESCRIPTION	UNIT PRICE	TOTAL
200	Gut Herlinghaus, Jahrgang 2010, Riesling Kabinett, 0.7 l	€7.35	€1,470.00

Normalerweise guter Kunde. Rechnung ist schon mehr als 4 Wochen überfällig. Bitte erinnern Sie Ms Greenway und schicken Sie eine Rechnungskopie als Anhang.
G. Roth

VAT % tax-exempt intra-Community delivery: not applicable

TERMS
30 days net

AMOUNT DUE €: 1,470.00

TITLE TO THE GOODS DESCRIBED ON THIS INVOICE DOES NOT PASS TO THE BUYER UNTIL THE INVOICE IS PAID IN FULL

8 Online research

Research the following topics and report your findings in class.

1. What is the Late Payment Directive of the European Union?
2. What is *factoring* and how does it work?

Replies to reminders

#basic reminder

When the customer receives a request for payment, he / she should either send the seller a letter of apology informing him / her that the amount is being paid or ask for an extension of time for payment. However, a buyer who is experiencing temporary payment difficulties should not wait until he receives a reminder, but should contact the seller, offer to pay in instalments and ask for a respite of the remaining amount.

1 Structure of a detailed reply to a reminder

a Match the different parts of a detailed reply to a reminder to the corresponding sentences (1 – 9) in the letter below.

apologies | explanation for the delay in payment | personal salutation | solution suggested: extension of due date, down payment and payment of balance at a later date, payment by instalments | reference to reminder(s) | appropriate ending | request for understanding | complimentary close | assurance that payment will be made

Dear Ms Osborne, [1]

We have received your email of 20 November concerning your statement of account No. UK/140-77 [2] and would like to offer our sincere apologies for the delay in payment. [3]

Unfortunately, three of our major customers have gone into compulsory liquidation in the last few months due to the general decline in the domestic tourism industry. This has obviously placed us in a somewhat precarious position. [4]
Due to these circumstances we would like to request a respite of three weeks. Alternatively, we could pay half of the sum now and the rest in four weeks' time. [5]

We hope you will understand our temporary predicament and see your way clear to granting us this concession, particularly in view of our long-standing business relations. [6]

You may be sure that we will be in a position to settle the account in the way suggested above, as we are expecting major payments from our overseas customers in the next few weeks. [7]

We are very sorry for the inconvenience caused and look forward to receiving your reply. [8]

Yours sincerely, [9]
...

b What is the purpose of the following sentences? Match the sentences (A – G) with the appropriate parts of a detailed reply to a reminder from exercise a.

- **A** We are expecting a considerable tax refund in the near future and this will enable us to meet our obligations in full.
- **B** Business has been slow recently and our own customers have been slow in paying their bills.
- **C** I am extremely sorry that the due date was overlooked by our accounts department.
- **D** Much to our regret we have to ask you for an extension of credit until 31 October.
- **E** We would suggest that we pay the invoice amount in three instalments of €7,500 each, due 10 June, 20 June and 30 June, respectively.
- **F** Having been a customer of yours for many years I am sure that you will agree to my proposal.
- **G** We acknowledge receipt of your letter dated 3 January reminding us that your invoice was due on 15 December.

2 Reactions to a reminder

Match the sentence parts and find out about possible reactions to a reminder. Note the collocations used.

1. Ideally, a customer should inform the supplier in good time about any difficulties he / she may be having in meeting …
2. He / she could then ask for …
3. In any case, a customer should apologise …
4. Should your company be unable to make payment in full, you will have to negotiate …
5. In the end, each side will have to make …
6. The customer could make …
7. Or he could agree on payment …

- **A** … a new payment plan with the supplier.
- **B** … for the delay.
- **C** … concessions.
- **D** … a respite.
- **E** … by instalments.
- **F** … his obligations.
- **G** … a down payment and pay the rest at a later date.

#skillletter **3 Writing a reply to a reminder**

D2 Letter

Die Firma Acoustic Empire (Nassauring 4, 60554 Frankfurt, Tel. +49 69 507 705 883…, acoustic-empire@easymail…com) hat die folgende Mahnung von Chords of Sorts (158 Clapham High St, London SW4 7ST) erhalten. Lesen Sie den Brief und die Notizen. Schreiben Sie dann eine angemessene Antwort.

In our letter of 20 August, we enclosed the invoice (AEDE G-39/4) for your order of 15 May (Your order No. 35-0513) for 20 T-Line electric bass guitars.

We have, however, not yet received payment of the outstanding amount of £ 5,385.00.

As you have been a reliable business partner for quite a few years we must assume that there are serious reasons for your not having remitted the above sum or contacted us regarding your delay in payment.

Please contact us as soon as possible to explain your reasons for withholding payment or arrange for prompt remittance of the amount to our usual account.

- *Ein Brand in unserer Zentrale hat unsere gesamte EDV-Anlage zerstört und auch wichtige Dateien vernichtet.*
- *Durch die enorme Zusatzarbeit, die dadurch entstanden ist, war unser Personal überlastet und konnte einige Zahlungstermine nicht einhalten.*
- *Die Kommunikation ist jetzt wieder ungestört und wir arbeiten sehr intensiv an der Erledigung der liegengebliebenen Kundenmitteilungen und Überweisungen.*
- *Bis Ende dieses Monats müsste der Betrag gutgeschrieben sein. Ein Rundschreiben an alle Kunden wird in den nächsten Tagen verschickt.*

! COMMON MISTAKES

1. We refer to our invoice ~~about/over~~ **amounting to** €715.20 ~~from~~ **of** 23 March.
2. Our invoice ~~about~~ **for** a consignment of books is still outstanding.
3. Please transfer ~~£ 25.750,50~~ **£ 25,750.50** to our account.
4. The invoice was due ~~at~~ **on** 31 July.
5. The account shows a balance of €65 ~~to~~ **in** our favour.
6. We suppose that you must have ~~overseen~~ **overlooked** our statement of account.
7. Please settle the account ~~until~~ **by** the end of the week.
8. The ~~due amount~~ **amount due** has already been remitted.
9. ~~In the last time~~ **Recently** we have also had problems collecting our outstanding accounts.
10. We suggest ~~to pay~~ **that we pay** in three ~~rates~~ **instalments** of £2,000 each.
11. We are, unfortunately, not in ~~the~~ **a** position to grant you the respite.
12. We trust you will agree ~~with~~ **to** our suggestions.

Business scenario

Im Rahmen Ihrer Ausbildung bei der Firma Garten Fröhlich GmbH, Römerstraße 150, 69117 Heidelberg, arbeiten Sie in der Buchhaltung. Garten Fröhlich vertreibt eine große Auswahl an Gartenzubehör. Vor fünf Wochen wurden Artikel im Wert von €12.500 an Rosegardens Ltd., 5 St. James St., Brighton BN2 1RE, England, geliefert. Es wurde vereinbart, dass die Bezahlung per Banküberweisung innerhalb von 30 Tagen mit einem Preisnachlass von 2% erfolgen sollte. Bis jetzt ist keine Zahlung eingegangen.

Step 1

#skill reminder

D11 Reminder

Ihre Vorgesetzte, Kirsten Hack, muss heute das Büro früher verlassen. Sie bittet Sie, eine Mahnung an die Firma zu schreiben und dabei ihre Hinweise in der Mail zu berücksichtigen.

Hallo …,
ich muss heute etwas früher gehen. Könnten Sie bitte eine freundliche Mahnung an die Firma Rosegardens mit den folgenden Angaben schicken. Kontakt ist Frau Doris Daisy (daisy@rosegardens…com). Unterschreiben Sie als mein/-e Assistent/-in.
- Bezug auf Lieferung vor 5 Wochen, Auftragsnummer RoGa 4711
- Freundliche Zahlungserinnerung, verweisen Sie auf das Zahlungsdatum
- Kopie der offenen Rechnung über 12.500 € beifügen

Danke.
Kirsten Hack

Step 2

Zwei Wochen später ist immer noch keine Zahlung eingegangen. Die Firma hat sich auch nicht gemeldet. Frau Hack bittet Sie eine zweite Mahnung per E-Mail zu schicken. Sie finden dazu eine Notiz von ihr auf Ihrem Schreibtisch.

- *Bezugnahme auf Rechnung von vor 7 Wochen und 1. Mahnung*
- *bisher hat sich die Firma weder gemeldet noch gezahlt*
- *Bitte um Erklärung des Zahlungsverzugs*
- *setzen Sie eine letzte Frist in 2 Wochen ab heute*

Step 3

A 20

Heute erreicht Sie der folgende Anruf. Erstellen Sie eine Gesprächsnotiz auf Deutsch für Frau Hack, die momentan in einer Besprechung ist und den Anruf nicht entgegennehmen kann.

Garten Fröhlich GmbH	Mr Wiffen
Guten Tag. Garten Fröhlich GmbH. Mein Name ist …	…
I'm sorry, she's in a meeting right now. Can I help you?	…
I'm sorry to hear that. Sorry, what was your name?	…
Okay, thanks, I've got that. And you are calling from Rosegardens, is that correct?	…
Okay, let me just get the file. And you say that the invoice has already been paid?	…
Well, we must have made a mistake somewhere. I have written down all the details for Ms Hack. I'm sure she'll be able to clear the matter up when she calls you back this afternoon. Will you be available?	…
Okay. Could I have the number, please?	…
Good, I've got that. She'll call you back later to tell you what's happened.	…
You're welcome. Goodbye	…

2 Kurzgefasste schriftliche Mitteilung (Bearbeitungszeit 30 Minuten)

Sie sind Sachbearbeiter/-in in der Rechnungsabteilung der Spielzeugfirma Kinderparadies in Ulm. Ihre Firma hat den beiliegenden Brief von der britischen Firma SuperTeddys Ltd erhalten. Ihr Chef, Christian Muigg, hat Ihnen den Brief zur Beantwortung gegeben und folgende Notiz daran geheftet:

Bitte schicken Sie in Ihrem Namen eine E-Mail (j.hamilton@superteddys...co.uk) zurück und unterschreiben Sie selbst. Erwähnen Sie folgende Punkte:

- *Vielen Dank, dass Sie uns rechtzeitig auf Ihre finanziellen Probleme aufmerksam gemacht haben.*
- *Selbstverständlich können wir den Zahlungstermin um 2 Wochen aufschieben. Wir wissen es zu schätzen, dass Sie Rechnungen immer pünktlich begleichen.*
- *Wir hoffen, dass die finanziellen Probleme Ihrer wichtigen Kunden inzwischen gelöst worden sind.*
- *Natürlich freuen wir uns auf Ihren nächsten Auftrag und fügen eine Broschüre zu einigen neuen Produkten bei.*
- *Vielen Dank!*

Kinderparadies
Herrn Christian Muigg
Regensburger Str.
89073 Ulm
GERMANY

SuperTeddys Ltd
37 The Level
Tunbridge Wells
Kent TN3 4PY
UK

3 June 20..

Dear Mr Muigg,

Your Invoice No. A7-3258 due 18 June 20..

I am writing to you before the above invoice is due as we may have difficulty settling it within the agreed timeframe.

I am afraid that a couple of our important customers have been in financial difficulties, and we have been forced to grant them respite. It seems that their financial situation is now improving.

However, to be on the safe side, I would like to ask you to allow us to postpone settlement of the above invoice by two weeks, i.e. to 1 July 20.. . I am very reluctant to ask this favour of you. We have always placed great value on settling invoices on time.

Thank you for your understanding.

Yours sincerely,
Jonathan Hamilton
Jonathan Hamilton
Sales Manager

3 Geschäftsbrief nach Stichworten (Bearbeitungszeit 45 Minuten)

Sie arbeiten im letzten Jahr Ihrer Berufsausbildung in der Rechnungsabteilung von The Bike Factory Europe GmbH, Zwickauer Str. 14 – 18, 04129 Leipzig, schon eigenverantwortlich. Die irische Firma Kerry Holidays LTD., 32 The Esplanade, Belfast AY1 33D, Nordirland, hat bei Ihnen am 26. März 20.. eine eilige Bestellung für 120 Fahrradhelme (Order Nr.: DE 342-33) zum Einkaufspreis von € 3845,50 platziert. Nachdem von Kerry Holidays LTD. eine Anzahlung von € 1000,00 geleistet wurde, ist die Ware geliefert worden. Laut Rechnung Nr. 210345 vom 2. April 20.. war der Restbetrag 10 Tage nach Warenerhalt fällig. Heute ist der 25. April 20.. und Ihrem Firmenkonto ist der Betrag noch nicht gutgeschrieben worden.

Mahnen Sie in einem Erinnerungsschreiben die ausstehende Summe an und beachten Sie dabei die folgenden Punkte:

- *Bezug auf den Auftrag vom ...*
- *Anfrage, ob die Sendung pünktlich gewesen und ohne Beanstandung ist*
- *Kopie der offenen Rechnung beifügen*
- *Verweisen Sie auf das Fälligkeitsdatum*
- *Zahlung per Banküberweisung auf Ihr Konto: DE56 4930 1220 0000 2324 25, BIC WSARO4ZR, bei der Sächsischen Handelsbank noch ausstehend*
- *Bitte Brief als gegenstandslos beachten, sollte die Zahlung bereits erfolgt sein*
- *Angemessener Schluss*

9 STARTER

MAKING ARRANGEMENTS

#basicarrangements

1 What experience do you have in making arrangements? Think of an example of something you have organised (e.g. a party, a trip or an event at your sports club) and tell your partner about it.

#basic arrangements 2 Create a word web about making arrangements in business. Choose an event, e.g. a supplier meeting or a sales pitch. What needs to be organised? Which companies are involved and who are the points of contact?

Organisational communication

Organisational communication is an essential part of working in administration: making appointments, communicating general information and coordinating arrangements are just a few of a wide range of possible tasks.

A 21 🔈 **1 Arranging a company visit**

#vocab meetings

Tom Schmitt, Sales Manager at The Bike Factory headquarters in Frankfurt, has found a potential new customer, Ruben Paterson, Head Buyer at DutchBikes in Amsterdam. Mr Paterson would like to see the company's premises and have an initial meeting with Tom. Tom's assistant, Sarah Hofmann, receives a phone call from Mr Paterson's assistant, Britt Janssen. She wants to arrange the meeting.

#skillmemo D3 Memo

As Sarah, take notes while you are listening and write a memo in German for Tom dated 1 October 20.. .

Sarah	Britt
Good afternoon, Sarah Hofmann, how can I help?	…
Hello Ms Janssen, how are you?	…
I'm fine too, thanks. Sure – I guess you are calling about Mr Paterson's visit. I saw in Mr Schmitt's inbox that he has arranged a meeting with him in two weeks' time.	…
Correct, he's asked Mr Paterson to join him for lunch and then take a look at the manufacturing site. I'm just checking his diary … he's put a blocker in for himself, but I'll send over an invitation for Mr Paterson too.	…
Oh yeah, that should be no problem. Although … I'm not sure if they're ready yet, I hear there have been problems with the delivery of some of the components. I'll check with Mr Schmitt.	…
Hm, again I'm not so sure. I guess it'll be no more than two hours but I'll ask Mr Schmitt and then get back to you. Regarding travel arrangements: can I ask, where will Mr Paterson be travelling from?	…
Yes, of course, no problem. I'll book him in as a visitor and arrange a parking space for him in the visitors' bay. I'll just need you to let me know the registration and the model of his car, please.	…
That'd be perfect, thanks. In fact, if you could also confirm his email address, then I can arrange internet access for him as well.	…
While I have you on the phone – does Mr Paterson have any special dietary requirements for the lunch?	…
OK, no problem, I'll tell Mr Schmitt to choose a restaurant that has good vegan options.	…
You're welcome. So I'll send over an invitation and the map shortly and I'll arrange a parking space and internet access once you've sent me his details. And if there's anything else in the meantime, just drop me a line.	…
No problem. Take care!	…

#skillemail
#vocab arrangements
D1 Email

2 Making appointments

In a team meeting, Tom Schmitt wants to discuss the company's involvement at the Sports Travel Fair in London. Since Miles Davies, Sales Manager at The Bike Factory's Cambridge office, will also be attending the fair, Tom would like Miles to join the planning meeting.

Read the email from Miles to Tom and the instructions Tom forwarded to his assistant, Sarah. Then write Tom's reply to Miles.

From: m.davies@thebikefactory…uk
To: t.schmitt@thebikefactory…de
CC: s.hofmann@thebikefactory…de
Subject: Sports Travel Fair meeting arrangements

Hi Tom,

Thanks for inviting us to the meeting. We would be very pleased to attend. It will give us the opportunity to discuss matters such as planning and coordination, logistics, optics, budget, who to invite and which products to promote. Working together from the start will be greatly beneficial, I am sure.
Unfortunately, neither of the dates you suggested are suitable as I have important meetings on both of those days. What about the week before or after? Would 24 November or 15 December work for you, for example?
Also, should we organise our own travel arrangements? If so, can you recommend a good hotel near our headquarters? I assume we will be meeting there.
Perhaps we can have dinner together the evening before the meeting? Would you be able to book a suitable place for us to go? There will be six of us coming from Cambridge.

All the best,
Miles

- *15.12. geht nicht (wichtiger Termin), also nehmen wir den 24.11.*
- *sollen Anreise selbst organisieren*
- *kann Red Box Business Hotel in Frankfurt empfehlen (5 Minuten entfernt, guter Service)*
- *Datum und Uhrzeit der An- und Abreise?*
- *Abendessen am Anreisetag im Asian Fusion – OK?*

Invitations

Team meetings often require no more than an informal invitation via email. Invitations to other teams, companies and customers, on the other hand, should be well thought out to ensure they contain all the necessary information for all participants. For particularly formal occasions, invitations should be sent by letter.

#vocab invitations
#skillemail

1 Meeting invitations

Miles and Tom found a suitable date for all attendees. Complete the invitation. There are 3 more words than you need.

arranged | attending | coming up | concerning | confirmation | delighted | happy | hold | jointly | lead | request | travel arrangements | warmly

From: s.hofmann@thebikefactory…de
To: The Bike Factory Cambridge
CC: j.torres@thebikefactory…uk
Subject: Meeting invitation 24 November

Dear colleagues,

As you all know, the Sports Travel Fair is **1** in March 20.. As teams from both the headquarters in Frankfurt and the offices in Cambridge will be **2** the fair, Tom and Miles would like to handle preparations **3** .
Therefore, we would be **4** to invite you to a joint preparatory meeting in Frankfurt on 24 November 20.., starting at 8 am. Tom and Miles will **5** the meeting.
6 will be organised by your assistant, Jane. She will be glad to help you with any questions **7** routes, timings etc.
Accommodation will be **8** for you at the Red Box Business Hotel in Frankfurt.
Upon your arrival on 23 November, you are **9** invited to dinner at the Asian Fusion restaurant at 6 pm.

We look forward to receiving **10** of your attendance.

All the best,
Sarah Hofmann, Team Assistant
The Bike Factory Frankfurt

#skillletter
#vocab exhibitions

2 Inviting visitors to a trade fair

Important (potential) commercial partners and customers should be personally invited to visit a company's booth or stand at a fair. This is a great opportunity to stand out from the competition.

a Use 20 of the following 23 words to complete the invitation on the next page.

admission | build | combining | contact | design | displayed | entirely | exhibition | first | happy | food | introducing | invite | main | of | opportunity | pattern | range | reason | specialise | stand | visit | well

Universal Box plc
Markgraf von der Lausitz-Allee 27
91003 Leipzig
Tel. +49 171 39200 50
k.stauder@universalbox...de
www.universalbox...com

02 January 20..

Dear ...,

Invitation: Packaging Design Fair in Mumbai
The Packaging Design Fair, where you are certain to find the latest designs in packaging as [1] as many other useful ideas, opens on 16 March in Mumbai. As you know, we [2] in packaging design for use in the [3] and beauty industries. This year we are [4] our new ECO [5] of recyclable plastic packaging solutions, which will be [6] for the [7] time in Mumbai. For this [8], we would like to personally [9] you to [10] our special display at [11] 17, in hall 3, near the [12] entrance. With ECO we have created an [13] new concept [14] expert craftmanship and state-of-the-art [15]. We hope you will not miss the [16] to see our new range for yourself. We will be more than [17] to offer you two complimentary [18] tickets for the packaging fair if you [19] us within four weeks [20] receiving this invitation.

We look forward to welcoming you at the fair.

Best wishes,
Universal Box plc

Katrin Stauder
for Martina Hegewald
Key Account Manager

#skillletter
#vocab meetings
D2 Letter

b As Sarah Hofmann (Team Assistant, The Bike Factory Frankfurt, Mainallee 123, 60306 Frankfurt), write a letter to Ruben Paterson (Head Buyer at DutchBikes, Schipperstraat 12-II, 1011 BB Amsterdam, NL), inviting him to visit The Bike Factory's stand at the Sports Travel Fair. Consider these notes from your supervisor (Tom Schmitt, Sales Manager).

- *Sports Travel Fair, Exhibition Centre London (ExCeL)*
- *3 – 5 March 20..*
- *Outdoor-Areal, Segment A4 Bike tours & Cycling vacations, Standnummer A4 – 129*
- *stellen unsere aktuelle Bikepacking-Linie aus: Cyclocross Bikes, Mountain Bikes und Touring Bikes, speziell hergestellt für längere Bikepacking-Touren; Bikepacking Accessoires (Taschen, Berg- und Campingequipment, Reparatursets u.v.m.)*
- *Tickets verfügbar für Herrn Paterson und 3 weitere Vertreter/-innen, bei Anfrage vor dem 15.01.*
- *unterschreiben Sie in meinem Namen*

Travel and bookings

Organising business trips often consists of hiring cars and booking tickets, hotels and exhibition stands. Although most of the bookings can be done online, personal communication is sometimes still necessary, e.g. when dealing with amendments, cancellations, or individual requests.

1 Individual requests

Melek Kaya from XYZ Travel is preparing to attend a tourism fair in Edinburgh. Complete her email to Skye Hotel, Edinburgh.

at | could | could not | during | have to | on | may | to | would (2 x) | would like to | would need

From: Melek Kaya
To: Skye Hotel Edinburgh
Date: 5 April 20..
Subject: Room reservation

Dear Sir or Madam,

I **1** reserve a room for three nights including breakfast from 29 April to 2 May. Unfortunately I **2** find a way to outline my specific requests **3** the online booking form, so I am including them in this email instead. As I arrive **4** 7 am, I **5** an early check-in, if that is possible. Also, I am allergic **6** dust mites so I would need one of your allergy-friendly rooms (as advertised on your website). I will probably **7** do some work **8** my stay, so I **9** need a desk. **10** that be possible?
I will be arriving on flight BA 542, which lands at 5:45 pm on 29 April. **11** you please arrange for an airport transfer?

Please **12** you confirm the booking? Let me know if you need any further information at all.

Many thanks.

Kind regards,
Melek Kaya

2 Cancelling a hotel reservation

#skill phonecall
#vocab phonecall
#vocabtravel

The tourism fair in Edinburgh has been moved to another exhibition centre. Melek Kaya needs to cancel her booking with the Skye Hotel since it is too far from the fair's new location. With a partner, act out the conversation between Melek and the hotel receptionist.
→ Role card B, p. 121

Role card A – Melek Kaya

- Sie arbeiten für das Unternehmen XYZ Travel in Berlin. Sie rufen im Skye Hotel in Edinburgh an. Sie haben für sich selbst ein Einzelzimmer vom 29. April bis zum 02. Mai gebucht. Die Konferenz, an der Sie teilnehmen werden, wurde in einen weiter entfernten Stadtteil verlegt, weshalb Sie die Buchung stornieren müssen.
- Sie möchten wissen, ob die bereits geleistete Anzahlung zurückerstattet wird und ob für die Stornierung eine Extragebühr erhoben wird.
- Sie möchten keinen Gutschein, sondern eine Rückerstattung.
- Bedanken Sie sich und beenden Sie das Gespräch.

3 Booking an exhibition stand

Katrin Stauder is Team Assistant at the Leipzig-based subsidiary of Universal Box plc, which has similar subsidiaries in other European countries. The company's head office is in Stockholm, Sweden, and the company language is English. Katrin's boss has asked her to arrange the company's participation at the Packaging Design Fair in Mumbai, India.

#vocab exhibitions

a Katrin calls Indira Chaudhary from the Mumbai Fairs Authority.
Act out the phone conversation with a partner. → Role card B, p. 121

Role card A – Katrin Stauder

- Begrüßen Sie Frau Chaudhary und stellen Sie sich und Ihr Anliegen kurz vor:
  Sie arbeiten für das Unternehmen Universal Box plc in Leipzig. Sie haben für Ihr Unternehmen vor 3 Wochen einen Stand gebucht und noch keine Bestätigung bekommen. Sie möchten den Status der Reservierung jetzt prüfen.
- Bedanken Sie sich für die Auskunft. Bitten Sie um eine Bestätigung per Mail.
- Nennen Sie Ihre Mailadresse:
  k.stauder@universalbox…de.
- Bedanken und verabschieden Sie sich.

A 22 **b** Katrin calls her counterpart, Angélique Villeneuve, in French-speaking Switzerland. Listen to their conversation. Take the role of Angélique (email address: a.villeneuve@universalbox…ch) and write an email to Katrin, giving her all the necessary information:
- flight number and time (flight number EK 048 arrives in Mumbai 5:45 pm local time)
- requires non-smoking room and vegetarian breakfast
- transport from airport and from hotel to exhibition centre?

4 Making hotel reservations for the fair

After having talked to Angélique, Katrin from Universal Box plc calls the Grand Mogul Palace Hotel in Mumbai. Rajiv Singh takes her call.

A 23 **a** Listen to the telephone conversation and take notes.

b Take the role of Katrin Stauder and send an email to Anna Parkanova (a.parkanova@universalbox…sk) in Bratislava informing her about the hotel arrangements, vegetarian options available etc. Ask her to book flights for her company executives and to confirm the details by email. The executives should arrive by 5 pm on 16 March.

#skillemail #vocabtravel

5 Hiring a rental car

Martina Cantillina is a trainee at Genshuber Maschinenbau GmbH in Bernau. Her supervisor is Olaf Brunner. She has just received a confirmation email from the rental car agency Car Hire Dublin, through which she has hired a car for Mr Brunner's trip to Dublin in a few weeks. Considering Mr Brunner's notes, write her reply to the agency.

From: booking@carhiredublin…ie
To: cantillina@gemabernau…de
CC: brunner@gemabernau…de
Date: 05 August 20..
Subject: Car Hire Booking Confirmation

Dear Ms Cantillina,
Thank you for choosing to book your car using www.carhiredublin…ie.
Your booking details are as follows:

Vehicle details Vehicle: Group C Offer includes: 5 doors, 5 seats Automatic Unlimited free kilometres Theft protection Registration fee	Confirmation number: 12345789 Insurance policy number: 12345ABC6789 **Price details** Rental period (2 days x €157.22) €314.44 Protection & extras €0 Total €314.44
Pick-up details Branch: Dublin City Centre Address: Dublin Car Hire House, 1234 Main Street, Dublin Phone: +353 1234 5678 Date: Monday, 17 August 20.. Time: 9 am	**Drop-off details** Branch: Dublin Airport Address: Dublin Car Hire Airport, 1234 Airport Street, Dublin Phone: +353 18765 432 Date: Wednesday, 19 August 20.. Time: 7 am

Client to pay on arrival with credit card.
Please contact booking@carhiredublin…ie if you have any questions regarding this booking.

- *brauche Wagen erst am nächsten Tag, dafür 3 Tage länger (hänge privaten Termin an den Besuch in Dublin an) – Preis?*
- *brauche größeren Kofferraum*
- *Wagen am Flughafen abholen, nicht im Stadtzentrum – OK?*
- *Möglichkeit, vor den offiziellen Öffnungszeiten Wagen abzugeben?*
- *vollgetankt zurückgeben?*

#skillemail
#vocabtravel
#vocab arrangements

6 Flight bookings

a Olaf Brunner is planning to fly from Zurich to London for a meeting with Mr Leigh from Cumbria Steel plc (email address: r.leigh@cumbria…uk). Study the excerpts from the timetable and the ticket, as well as Mr Brunner's notes to Martina Cantillina, the trainee (cantillina@gemabernau…de). Write Martina's email.

- *alle wichtigen Flugdaten bitte an Mr Leigh*
- *nehme Taxi vom Flughafen London Heathrow zum Hotel The Londoner*
- *Treffen in Hotellobby um 12 Uhr – gemeinsames Mittagessen?*

DEPARTURES ZURICH ZRH LONDON LHR

TIME	FLIGHT	REMARKS
07:05 – 07:55	BA 713	on schedule
07:30 – 09:05	LX 316	on schedule
14:30 – 16:00	LX 464	on schedule

BOARDING PASS

NAME OF PASSENGER	FLIGHT NO.	SEAT	DATE
Olaf Brunner	LX 316	37A	20 Aug

FROM	TO	DEPARTURE TIME	GATE
ZURICH / ZRH	LONDON / LHR	07:30	415

Check your final gate information

NAME OF PASSENGER		DATE
Olaf Brunner		20 Aug
FROM	**TO**	**FLIGHT NO.**
ZURICH / ZRH	LONDON / LHR	LX 316
BOARDING TIME	**SEAT**	**GATE**
06:50	37A	415

A 24
#skillmemo
D3 Memo

b Mr Brunner's return flight was cancelled at short notice. He asked Martina to call the airline and figure out his options. Listen to the conversation (date: 21 August). As Martina, write a memo for Mr Brunner.

Martina	Daniel
Hello there, my name is Martina Cantillina. I'm calling from Genshuber Maschinenbau on behalf of my boss – he had a flight from London to Zurich booked for tomorrow evening but he's just called and told me that it's been cancelled! Please can you confirm the status of the flight?	…
Yes, it's Olaf Brunner and the flight was LX 327 from London Heathrow to Zurich, departing at 6:40 pm.	…
Oh, I see. OK. What options do we have for rebooking?	…
No, that won't work, he has an important meeting that day starting at 9:00 am. He really needs to fly back tomorrow evening. Is there nothing else available?	…
Today … hmm. I'm not sure – I'll need to speak to Mr Brunner and check with him. I'll give you a call back once I've got in touch with him. That's our only option, if I've understood correctly?	…
Alright. Thanks for your help. I'll speak to Mr Brunner right away and let you know.	…
Goodbye.	…

Business scenario

#vocab conferences

You work for XYZ Travel. Your company is hosting a conference in your city and has invited international commercial partners and potential customers to take part. Your supervisor, Ines Müller, has asked you to make arrangements for two important customers.

Step 1 #basic arrangements

Read the email from Steve Holmes, Key Account Manager at XYZ Travel Global, a subsidiary in the US, and the profiles of the international visitors. Note relevant keywords and write a memo in German for your supervisor, Ines. Date: 28 July 20..

Dear Ines,
Thanks for taking care of our most important clients. I just wanted to give you a few more details to help you make your suggestions, so I have included a brief profile of Ms Adebisi and Mr Hasebe below. The conference schedule finishes on Friday afternoon at 4 pm and the guests are staying until Saturday. It is important that any activities are completed by around 5:30 pm on Saturday as Ms Adebisi needs to be back at the airport by 7 pm. Although we want to make their stay as special as possible, we do have a budget. I have been told that you will have around € 1,200 to play with, so see if you can make that work.
I am looking forward to seeing what you come up with.

Regards,
Steve Holmes

Ms Nikki Adebisi, South Africa
(Purchasing Executive, African Adventure Tours)

- fitness fanatic who loves being outdoors
- has never been to Germany before
- needs a gift for her teenage daughter
- wants to see the 'real Germany'

Mr Takashi Hasebe, Japan
(CEO, Nagoya Smart City Project)

- loves good food and fine wines
- likes shopping, culture and the arts
- has only been to Germany once before
- not very sporty

Step 2 #basic arrangements

Research appropriate activity suggestions in your city for Friday after 4 pm and all day Saturday until 5:30 pm (budget: € 1,200).

Step 3 #skillemail #vocabemail

Write an email to the guests informing them of the final plans (your email address: yourname@xyztravel…de). Consider these notes from your boss, Ines.

- *Mail in meinem Namen an Nikki Adebisi (adebisi@aat...za) und Takashi Hasebe (hasebe@smartcity...jp), mich in CC (mueller@xyztravel...de)*
- *freuen uns auf ihren Besuch und unser Kennenlernen*
- *erkläre, welche Freizeitaktivitäten wir für ihren Aufenthalt geplant haben – alle einverstanden?*
- *Catering und Restaurants: Allergien, Ernährungsweisen?*
- *Konferenzplan anhängen*
- *bei Fragen an dich wenden*

Review

Before you test yourself in *Exam practice*, take a few moments to reflect on what you have just learned. Then make a follow-up plan: What do you need to improve before the final exam? How will you go about getting there? You can check again after *Exam practice*.

#basic arrangements

In this unit, you have learned how to ...
pass on general information | make appointments for visits and meetings | write invitations | book hotels, flights etc. | book an exhibition stand

1 Considering these topics and tasks, ask yourself:

#vocab meetings
#vocab exhibitions
#vocab conferences
#vocabtravel
#vocabemail
#gramtenses
#gram prepositions
#skillemail
#skillletter
#skill phonecall
#skillmemo

Vocabulary	Do I know the relevant words and phrases needed to ... arrange meetings | book hotels, flights etc. | organise and book an exhibition stand | write invitations | pass on general information?
	Can I understand and use these relevant words and phrases confidently in speaking and in writing?
	Can I adapt my language to the medium / channel I use (letter, email, phone) and the addressee (boss, colleague, stranger, someone I know ...)?
Grammar	When writing and / or speaking, did I come across a common source of grammar mistakes? If so, what was it and how can I practise and improve in this particular area?
Writing	Do I know how to structure a formal letter / email?
	What do I need to consider when writing a business letter / email, e.g. an invitation or a stand booking?
	What do I need to consider when writing a memo, e.g. about arranging a company visit?
	What do I need to consider when passing on general information like a change of address?
Speaking	Can I confidently express my concerns over the phone when it comes to meetings and bookings, e.g. confirmations and cancellations?
Methods / Strategies	Do I know how to distinguish relevant information from irrelevant information, e.g. when taking notes during a phone call?

2 Use your answers from 1 to create a learning and revision plan.

WHAT? What do I need to work on?	**HOW?** What will I do to improve?	**WHEN?** When do I want to complete this?
...	...	...

TIP
Watching series, reading books and listening to podcasts in English can greatly improve your understanding of the English language. Try to make it a habit if you want to work on your general language skills.

Exam practice

Mündliche Prüfung: Telefongespräch (Dauer ca. 20 Minuten)

Üben Sie gemeinsam mit einem Partner / einer Partnerin.
Tauschen Sie nach einem Durchgang die Rollen.

Partner A (Kandidat/-in):
Sie sind Teamassistent/-in bei der Firma Astroglobe GmbH in Meissen. Die Leiterin Ihrer Abteilung, Annette Pollnow, wird nächste Woche einen Geschäftspartner in Hongkong besuchen. Da sie heute noch ein wichtiges Meeting hat, hat sie Ihnen folgende E-Mail geschickt. → Role card B, p. 121

Liebe/-r …

bitte rufen Sie die Assistentin von Wong Lee Instruments in Hongkong an und teilen ihr die Einzelheiten über meinen Besuch nächste Woche mit.
Bitte fragen Sie nach dem Namen des Leiters der Forschungsabteilung, mit dem ich mich am Mittwoch treffen werde und lassen Sie sich den Namen buchstabieren. Bitte fragen Sie auch nach, wie lange die Besprechung mit Herrn Wu-Dziao am Donnerstag dauern wird und ob ich noch Zeit für eine Stadtrundfahrt einplanen kann.
Ich hätte auch gern gewusst, ob es möglich ist, dass mich jemand vom Flughafen abholt.
Ich hänge Ihnen meinen Terminplan als Excel-Datei an.

Vielen Dank
Annette Pollnow

Anhang:

20	Mittwoch	21	Donnerstag
08.00	Ankunft Hongkong 8.22, LH 330	10.00	Treffen mit Mr Wu-Dziao
11.00	Treffen mit Mr (?), Forschungsabteilung	18.00	Rückflug 18.12 nach Frankfurt, LH 320
14.00	Besichtigung der Labors von Wong Lee		
16.00	Besuch der neuen Ausbildungsakademie		
19.00	Essen mit Isabel Sing		

10 STARTER

#basicapplications APPLICATIONS

1 Knowing and understanding your skills, strengths and weaknesses is essential to finding the right job and convincing an employer to hire you. What are your key competencies? Share your ideas with a partner. Then make a list of the points you would wish to bring to the attention of a potential employer in a job application.

2 There are often several stages involved in a recruitment process, each of which might involve different documents from both the applicant and the employer. Brainstorm the stages of a job application. For each one, take brief notes on what happens, who is involved and which documents might be provided from each party.

Job advertisements

Job advertisements provide hints about what an employer is looking for in the ideal candidate. You can often take the words and phrases used in an advertisement and reuse them in your application documents.

1 Parts of a job advertisement

a Read the following advertisement. Match the different parts of a job advertisement to the corresponding sections (1–6).

summary of company and role | position | salary and working hours | benefits | application requirements and contact details | skills and requirements

IT Customer Support Officer [1]

As an e-commerce company with clients worldwide, we are on the lookout for an IT Customer Support Officer to assist our customers with any technical challenges they may have. [2]

We are interested in English speakers with great communication skills and excellent knowledge of a range of e-commerce software and administration programmes. Ideally, you will have studied IT and have some experience working within the field. [3]

We offer fixed weekly working hours and an initial starting salary of €22,000 per annum. [4] We place high value on a great working environment: you will work in bright, airy offices with access to a subsidised company cafeteria. [5]

If this sounds like your next role, please submit a CV and cover letter to jobs@k-info...de by 31 July 20... [6]

b Complete the job advertisement with the phrases from the box.

into practice | documentation | personnel | efficiently | as and when | shifts | hourly rate | member | interpersonal | manage | processing and coordination | organised

Logistics Coordinator

We are looking for a dynamic new [1] of our logistics team to assist with the [2] of international customer orders. Put your knowledge [3] and take the lead in helping to [4] the warehouse and exports!

You should be able to work [5] and independently and have excellent communication and [6] skills. At the same time, you should be highly [7] and proactive in solving problems [8] they arise. You will also be responsible for written [9].
Our logistics [10] work [11] totalling between 15 and 40 hours per week, they are paid an [12] of €13.50.

Please send your application to a-z.logistics@...de by midnight on 21 October 20...

Application documents

#basic applications

A CV is almost always required as part of a job application. When applying for a job in English, it is important to be aware of the differences between a German *Lebenslauf* and an English CV.

1 German *Lebenslauf* vs. English CV

Read the short text about writing a CV in English. Then explain to a partner: What would you do differently when compiling a CV for a German or English employer?

> Try to keep your CV brief and concise – one page if possible, or no more than two. Make sure to write down your work experience, education and qualifications in reverse chronological order and include any skills and interests which are relevant to the job. Alter any German terms (e.g. qualifications or job titles) into English equivalents.
>
> When applying for a job in the UK, you should not include a photo or your marital status and you do not need to sign your name at the end. You also do not necessarily need to give a testimonial – if an employer wants references, they will ask you for these separately.

2 Putting together a CV

A25

#skillcv

a Listen carefully and take notes about:

1. points to include in a CV
2. education details
3. work experience details
4. skills

#skillmemo D3 Memo

b Write a memo in German about the structure and contents of an English CV.

D12 CV

c Use the template and your notes from the previous exercise to create your own CV.

3 Writing a cover letter

#skill coverletter

A cover letter accompanies a CV and gives you the chance to explain to the employer in more detail why you are interested in the company and the position, and why you are suitable for it.

#gramtenses

a The following sentences might be used in a cover letter. Complete the sentences with the correct conjugation of the words and phrases from the box. There are two more than you need.

to have | to be interested in | to work | to look for | to be | to develop | to do | to graduate | to play | to get | to join

1. I **1** a hard-working, reliable and motivated individual.
2. I **2** a position in which I can **3** my communication skills.
3. I **4** working for your company because it is innovative and forward-thinking.
4. Currently I **5** an apprenticeship in bookkeeping.
5. I **6** previous work experience as a sales assistant.
6. After leaving school, I **7** a part-time job at a bakery.
7. I **8** for a small travel agency for the past eighteen months.
8. I **9** from college with a qualification in business administration.

#gram prepositions

b Read the following extract from a cover letter. Complete the gaps with the correct preposition.

at (2x) | as (2x) | with | in (3x) | to

I studied Business Management 1 Freiburg Vocational College and graduated in 2014. During my studies, I also completed a six-month internship 2 a bank clerk, where I supported the bank manager 3 administrative tasks. [1]

Since completing my studies, I have been working 4 a secretary 5 a small private law firm 6 Frankfurt. This has enabled me to gain considerable experience 7 the legal sector and improve my organisation and office communications skills. [2]

I am looking for a position in which I can develop the skills and expertise I have gained so far. I am particularly interested 8 working for your company because of its long-standing knowledge and expertise in corporate and business law. I am also attracted 9 its positive and friendly working atmosphere. [3]

c Match the parts of a cover letter to the corresponding sections in the extract above (1–3).

vision of future role | education and training | work experience

D13 Cover letter

d Look back at the example job advertisements on page 111 or go online and look for a position which interests you. Using the template and the previous exercises, write a cover letter for the job.

Interviews

Whether an interview takes place on the phone, online or in person, it is important to prepare well for it in advance. While this may differ slightly depending on whether it'll be a traditional or virtual meeting, the structure of an interview is generally standard.

#skill interview

1 Structure of a job interview

a Look at the following elements of a job interview. Arrange each one into the correct category of the table to say who is responsible for it: the interviewer, the candidate, or both.

Interviewer	Candidate	Both
…	…	…

1. questions to the employer
2. questions to the candidate
3. discussion about salary
4. reasons for application
5. welcome and introduction
6. summary of personal profile, background, experience etc.
7. short presentation of the company
8. summary of job role and responsibilities
9. information about next steps

b Arrange the elements 1.–9. into a logical order as you would expect them to come up in an interview conversation.

2 Preparing for an interview

a Read the tips about how to prepare for an interview. Can you think of any more? Discuss ideas in class.

DO
… research the company, its products and the job role and responsibilities.
… have your documents and notes to hand – your CV, cover letter, your questions written down and a pen and paper to take notes.
… practise answering questions the interviewer might ask you, on your own or with a friend or family member.
… check your equipment is working properly beforehand and use a quiet and tidy space where you won't be interrupted, if your interview is online.

DON'T
… interrupt the interviewer – always let them finish their sentence or question before you start speaking.
… dress in clothes that are too casual.
… speak too quickly or talk about things that aren't relevant to the question asked.
… be afraid to ask the interviewer to repeat themselves if you didn't hear or understand.
… worry if you have to take a few moments to think about your answer before you respond.

A 26 b Listen to the podcast with the manager of a careers agency and answer the questions.

1. What does Luke say is the best way to handle nerves before a job interview?
2. According to Luke, what is the point of unusual, abstract questions in a job interview?
3. Which tips does Luke give for a video interview?

c Match the terms to form a list of things needed for an online interview.

1 stable | **2** quiet room | **3** digital device | **4** video conferencing | **5** smart, formal

A software | **B** clothing | **C** without distractions | **D** internet connection | **E** with a camera and microphone

3 Interview questions

a Go online and search for the top 10 most common interview questions. Take notes and write down ideas about how you would answer the questions.

#gram adjectives
#gram adverbs

b In a job interview, a candidate is asked about their strengths. Read the response and identify the adjectives and adverbs.

> I am a great communicator and team player, but I also work well independently. I am very hard-working and although I don't yet have much experience in this particular field, I learn quickly. I understand that this position calls for somebody who is both creative and innovative, as well as resilient and able to make rational decisions, even in stressful situations.

c Match the words from the text above to their German equivalents.

1 independently | **2** yet | **3** field | **4** to call for | **5** resilient | **6** rational

A vernünftig | **B** Bereich | **C** bislang | **D** widerstandsfähig | **E** unabhängig | **F** benötigen

4 Role play: Job interview in English

#vocab applications

Work in pairs. Choose one of the job advertisements on page 111 or go online and find an interesting position. Conduct a job interview for the position, using the structure and phrases below for guidance.

Interviewer	Candidate
Greet the candidate, thank them for meeting you and make polite small talk.	Greet the interviewer in return, thank them for the invitation and make polite small talk.
Offer a brief introduction and outline of the company and role and ask the candidate why they are interested in the position.	Introduce yourself, give your reasons for applying and say what interests you about the job and the company.
Ask the candidate what makes them suitable for the position – check qualifications, experience, skills and personal qualities.	Summarise your relevant qualifications and experience, talk about your skills and personal qualities and say how these things would enable you to contribute to the role.
Ask the candidate if they have any questions about the company, role or responsibilities.	Ask about the company, role, working environment etc. and about the next stages of the recruitment process.
Explain what will happen next and thank the candidate for their time.	Express your interest in the role again and thank the employer for the opportunity to meet them and introduce yourself.

Review

Before you test yourself in *Exam practice*, take a few moments to reflect on what you have just learned. Then make a follow-up plan: What do you need to improve before the final exam? How will you go about getting there? You can check again after *Exam practice*.

#basic applications

In this unit, you have learned how to ...
understand a job advertisement | put together a CV | write a cover letter | structure a job interview | prepare for an interview | take part in a job interview in English

1 Considering these topics and tasks, ask yourself:

#vocab applications	**Vocabulary**	Do I know the relevant words and phrases needed to ... understand a job advertisement | put together a CV | write a cover letter | structure a job interview | prepare for an interview | take part in a job interview in English?
		Can I understand these relevant words and phrases confidently in reading and listening and use them in speaking and in writing?
#gramtenses #gram adjectives #gramadverbs	**Grammar**	When writing and / or speaking, did I come across a common source of grammar mistakes? If so, what was it and how can I practise and improve in this particular area?
#skillcv	**Writing**	Do I know how to structure a CV?
#skill coverletter		Do I know how to write a cover letter?
#skill interview	**Speaking**	Can I answer interview questions and take part in a job interview?
	Methods / Strategies	Can I understand a job advertisement to prepare an application accordingly? Can I anticipate what might come up in a job interview and prepare accordingly?

2 Use your answers from 1 to create a learning and revision plan.

WHAT? What do I need to work on?	**HOW?** What will I do to improve?	**WHEN?** When do I want to complete this?
...	...	...

TIP

If you are applying for several positions at once, you can often reuse the documents that you've already prepared. Make sure to adapt the relevant parts so that they fit to each role and company – especially in the cover letter.

Exam practice

1 Bewerbungsunterlagen in der Fremdsprache (Bearbeitungszeit 45 Minuten)

Verfassen Sie ein Bewerbungsschreiben auf Englisch für die ausgeschriebene Stelle. Denken Sie an Informationen zu Ihrer Person, Ausbildung, Erfahrungen und Eignung für die Position.

Internship: Events coordinator
Do you have strong organisational skills and a good eye for detail? Do you enjoy working in a team? Then this could be the job for you! JamBrite Events is an international events agency with clients across Europe. We are looking for a self-motivated individual to support the events management team with coordination and administrative tasks. You will be responsible for booking suppliers, arranging meetings and keeping the accounts, files and day-to-day office processes running smoothly. You should be able to work efficiently within a fast-paced environment and have exceptional communication skills. If this sounds like the internship for you, please send your application documents to m.pollini@jambrite… by 28 April 20...

A 27 ◁))

2 Vermerk über ein Telefongespräch (Bearbeitungszeit 20 Minuten)

Im folgenden Gespräch sind Sie Martina Pollini von der Firma JamBrite Events. Sie führen ein Telefongespräch mit Joshua Bell, einem potenziellen Praktikanten. Verfolgen Sie das Gespräch und fertigen Sie für die Personalabteilung eine Gesprächsnotiz auf Deutsch an.

Martina Pollini	Joshua
Hi Joshua, this is Martina Pollini calling from JamBrite Events.	…
I'm also glad to discuss your application! So, perhaps you could start off by telling me what interests you in the internship at JamBrite?	…
Right, OK! And do you have any experience in the event management industry?	…
Great – that sounds interesting. So, Joshua, what would you say are your greatest strengths and weaknesses?	…
It all counts! And your weaknesses?	…
I see. That's actually an important skill in events management, but it's also something you can pick up and improve with practice. Now, do you have any questions you want to ask me, Joshua?	…
Right. Well, to begin with, you'd be working alongside Tina, an experienced event manager. Tina has a large contact pool of various freelancers who provide the different services that make up a successful event. She usually has 3 or 4 projects on the go, so she'll be sure to keep you busy!	…
We have a few more candidates to speak to, but you'll hear from us with our decision within the coming fortnight.	…
You're more than welcome. Thanks for your time, Joshua. Speak to you soon.	…

ROLE CARDS

UNIT 3

Offers

Business scenario, Step 2

→ Role card A: see page 32

Role card B – Lantbruk, Stockholm, Schweden

- Nehmen Sie den Telefonanruf eines deutschen Landmaschinenherstellers an.
- Sie interessieren sich für den Vertrieb der deutschen Maschinen, da deutsche Landmaschinen einen guten Ruf haben. Sie brauchen allerdings mehr Informationen und fragen nach einer möglichen Vorführung der verschiedenen Maschinen.
- Verabreden Sie sich zu einem Verhandlungsgespräch, wo mögliche Themen wie Lieferung, Service, Bezahlung etc. besprochen werden können.
- Legen Sie gemeinsam Zeitpunkt und Dauer des Besuchs fest.
- Sie freuen sich sehr über die Übernahme der Reisekosten durch die deutsche Firma.
- Sie möchten alle besprochenen Details per E-Mail erhalten und werden eine Bestätigung Ihrer Reisedaten zusenden.
- Verabschieden Sie sich angemessen.

UNIT 4

Orders

Business scenario, Step 1

→ Role card A: see page 44

Role card B – Sono Inc., Janice Stevens, Sales Europe

- Nehmen Sie den Anruf entgegen.
- Sie sind für den Verkauf von 3D-Druckern zuständig.
- Ihre Firma hat bereits Erfahrung auf dem Gebiet. Fragen Sie, wie AEP auf Ihre Firma gekommen ist.
- Nennen Sie die Preise Ihrer 3D-Drucker: je nach Model zwischen 3.000 und 8.000 US-Dollar.
- Lieferung eines Testgeräts ist kein Problem, die Arbeitseinweisung könnte via Webkonferenz stattfinden.
- Fragen Sie, wie viele Geräte AEP eventuell im Anschluss bestellen würde.
- Sagen Sie, dass Sie direkt nach Bestelleingang liefern können.
- Verabschieden Sie sich angemessen.

UNIT 5

Delivery

Business scenario, Step 3

Role card A – Baumaschinen KG, Hamburg

- Rufen Sie bei Kuma Mining Germany an.
- Stellen Sie sich als Assistent/-in von Herrn Bistram vor.
- Erklären Sie, dass sich die Lieferung der bestellten Ersatzteile verzögern wird.
- Erklären Sie Herrn Kumari die möglichen Alternativen.
- Versichern Sie dem Kunden, dass Sie alles tun werden, um eine Lösung zu finden, damit die Ersatzteile so schnell wie möglich ausgeliefert werden können. Weisen Sie auf höhere Gewalt hin.
- Laden Sie Herrn Kumari ein, Ihre Produktionsstätte in Hamburg zu besuchen.
- Fragen Sie nach einem Termin.
- Entschuldigen Sie sich für die Verzögerung und beenden Sie das Gespräch freundlich.

Role card B – Herr Kumari, Kuma Mining Germany

- Nehmen Sie den Anruf entgegen.
- Lassen Sie sich den Namen buchstabieren und fragen Sie, worum es geht.
- Sie sind entsetzt, da Sie die Teile dringend benötigen.
- Betonen Sie, dass die Ersatzteile schnellstmöglich geliefert werden müssen, da sonst ein Produktionsstillstand droht.
- Bedanken Sie sich für das Engagement eine schnelle Lösung zu finden und bitten Sie darum, dass man Sie auf dem Laufenden hält.
- Gute Idee. Sie würden das Werk gerne besichtigen.
- Sie werden sich direkt mit Herrn Bistram in Verbindung setzen und mit ihm einen Termin vereinbaren.
- Beenden Sie das Gespräch mit einem freundlichen Schluss.

UNIT 6

Payment

Business scenario, Step 2

→ Role card A: see page 67

Role Card B – Ole Sörensen, Lantbruk AB

- Rufen Sie bei der Firma Sorglos GmbH an.
- Erklären Sie, dass Sie eine Frage zur Rechnung Nr. R-5834-23 haben.
- Sagen Sie, dass die Rechnung von der Buchhaltung Ihrer Firma bereits bezahlt wurde, und Sie leider erst jetzt bemerkt haben, dass in der Rechnung kein Einführungsrabatt berücksichtigt worden ist. Sie erinnern daran, dass bei Ihrem Besuch in Hannover ein Einführungsrabatt von 5% in Aussicht gestellt wurde.
- Nehmen Sie die Entschuldigung an und fragen Sie, wie nun weiter verfahren wird.
- Akzeptieren Sie den Vorschlag.
- Bedanken Sie sich und kündigen Sie weitere Bestellungen an. Verabschieden Sie sich angemessen.

Exam practice, Aufgabe 3

→ Role card A: see page 71

Role card B – Prüfer/-in

- You are George O'Connor of GIVIX LTD.
- You are taking the call from SAS Print GmbH regarding the reminder for invoice R-186-1002/02.
- Your accounts department transferred the amount of 2,450.00 € (2,500.00 € less 2 % early payment discount) to the account given at Commerzbank Duisburg.
- You suggest checking the IBAN. The IBAN stated on the invoice is DE38 3504 0085 0134 3132 13.
- After finding out that this number was not correct, you accept the apologies and a payment discount of 5 %.

UNIT 7

Complaints and adjustments

Business scenario, Step 2

→ Role card A: see page 80

Role card B – Nancy McMara, Cycling Ltd., Belfast

- Nehmen Sie den Anruf von The Bike Factory entgegen.
- Fragen Sie, wie es Richard Becker geht.
- Beschreiben Sie nochmals kurz, was das Problem mit der Lieferung war. Erklären Sie höflich, aber bestimmt, dass es für Sie wichtig ist, darauf vertrauen zu können, dass Bestellungen sorgfältig und korrekt ausgeführt werden.
- Erinnern Sie daran, dass Sie die T-Shirts dringend benötigen.
- Fragen Sie, was Sie mit den falsch gelieferten T-Shirts machen sollen. Sie können nicht alle T-Shirts behalten.
- Stimmen Sie dem angebotenen Rabatt zu.
- Bitten Sie den / die Anrufer/-in seinen / ihren Namen zu buchstabieren.
- Sie sind froh, dass die Sache so schnell geklärt werden konnte. Sie richten herzliche Grüße an Richard Becker aus und verabschieden sich.

UNIT 9

Making arrangements

Workshop C, Aufgabe 2

→ Role card A: see page 103

Role card B – Hotel receptionist, Skye Hotel, Edinburgh

- Sie arbeiten als Rezeptionist/-in im Skye Hotel in Edinburgh. Sie erhalten einen Anruf von Melek Kaya.
- Bitten Sie Melek Kaya, Namen und Details der Reservierung zu wiederholen.
- Für die Stornierung wird keine Gebühr berechnet, da die Stornierung rechtzeitig erfolgt ist. Eine Gebühr wird nur im Falle einer späten Stornierung erhoben. Für die bereits geleistete Zahlung bieten Sie einen Gutschein an.
- Sie werden die Rückerstattung veranlassen.
- Verabschieden Sie sich höflich.

Workshop C, Aufgabe 3 a

→ Role card A: see page 104

Role card B – Indira Chaudhary

- Melden Sie sich am Telefon.
- Bitten Sie um einen Moment Zeit, um im Buchungssystem nachzuschauen.
  Bestätigen Sie dann die Standbuchung: Eckstand, 25m², mit separatem Konferenzbereich.
- Fragen Sie nach der Mailadresse.
- Wiederholen Sie die Mailadresse. Kündigen Sie an, die Bestätigung so schnell wie möglich zu senden.
- Bedanken und verabschieden Sie sich.

Exam practice

→ Role card A: see page 109

Role card B – Prüfer/-in

- You are Christine Dong of Wong Lee Instruments in Hong Kong and work as an assistant to Mr Wu (European customer liaison officer).
- Someone from Astroglobe GmbH in Meissen, Germany, calls you to discuss Ms Pollnow's forthcoming visit to Wong Lee Instruments and to give flight details.
- Tell the caller that you will arrange to have Ms Pollnow picked up from the airport at around 8.45 am. Depending on the traffic, it may take a bit longer. The driver will carry a sign with the company's name on it.
- Head of the research department is Harry Zuang-Wu.
- The meeting with Mr Wu-Dziao is scheduled from 10 am to around 1 pm. Mr Wu-Dziao was hoping to have lunch with Ms Pollnow after the meeting. Ask the caller if Ms Pollnow could do the city sightseeing tour on the Wednesday.

HINWEISE ZU DEN PRÜFUNGSTEILEN

Zusatzqualifikation Englisch für kaufmännische Auszubildende

Schriftliche Prüfung

1 Geschäftsbrief nach Stichworten

§2 (2) a) der Rechtsvorschrift – Richtzeit: 45 Minuten

Es muss ein vollständiger, unterschriftsreifer Geschäftsbrief nach vorgegebenen Stichworten verfasst werden, mit Absenderadresse, Anschrift (mit Länderangabe und evtl. Namen des Empfängers), Datum, Anrede, Betreff, Grußformel, Namen und Position des Unterzeichners und gegebenenfalls Anlagevermerk. In seiner äußeren Form soll der Brief je nach Empfänger englischen oder amerikanischen Gepflogenheiten entsprechen. Das erste Wort einer englischen Korrespondenz wird groß geschrieben.
Ein allgemeines, zweisprachiges Wörterbuch ist erlaubt, muss aber mitgebracht werden.
Alle unter den beiden Rubriken **Situation** und **Aufgabe** enthaltenen relevanten Angaben sind in den Brief einzubeziehen. Die Stichwortangaben sollten jedoch möglichst nicht übersetzt, sondern mit Hilfe der kaufmännischen *terms and phrases* zu einem selbständig formulierten Brief verarbeitet werden.
Da bei der Beurteilung des Inhalts eines Geschäftsbriefs neben den Kriterien **sachliche Richtigkeit**, **inhaltliche Vollständigkeit** und **Gedankenführung** (Gliederung) auch die Punkte **Situationsangemessenheit** und **Wirkung** eine Rolle spielen, sollte darauf geachtet werden, dass der richtige Ton getroffen wird, z. B. kundenbezogen-freundlich bei einem Angebot, sachlich-drängend im Falle einer Mahnung. Man darf jedoch nicht außer Acht lassen, dass englischsprachige Geschäftskorrespondenz in der Regel verbindlicher formuliert wird als deutsche.

2 Kurzgefasste Mitteilung per moderner Telekommunikation (E-Mail)

§2 (2) b) der Rechtsvorschrift – Richtzeit: 30 Minuten

Auf die fremdsprachige Vorlage (E-Mail, Fax, Brief, Memo, Rechnung u. ä.) muss mit Hilfe von deutschen Stichwortangaben angemessen, d. h. nicht nur inhaltlich korrekt, sondern auch in entsprechendem Ton unter Beachtung der durch die Vorlage vorgegebenen Anrede (evtl. Vornamen) und Grußformel reagiert werden. Es empfiehlt sich, die Vorlage sorgfältig zu lesen, sie kann nützliche Vokabeln und Wendungen enthalten. In Übereinstimmung mit der englischen Vorlage kann ein informeller Stil unter Verwendung von Zusammenziehungen (*don't*, *we'd* etc.) und allgemein gebräuchlichen Abkürzungen (*asap*, *pls* etc.) angebracht sein. Beim Ausfüllen eines vorgegebenen Formblatts für die Mitteilung ist auf Vollständigkeit zu achten, vor allem der Betreff darf nicht übersehen werden. Ein allgemeines zweisprachiges Wörterbuch darf benutzt werden.

3 Vermerk in Deutsch über ein in der Fremdsprache geführtes Telefongespräch

§2 (2) c) der Rechtsvorschrift – Richtzeit ausschließlich Aufgabendarbietung: 20 Minuten

Die zu prüfenden Personen erhalten eine Situationsbeschreibung mit Aufgabe. Dann wird ein Telefongespräch zweimal zu Gehör gebracht. Was der deutsche Gesprächsteilnehmer auf Englisch sagt, liegt schriftlich vor. In diese Vorlage dürfen während des Gesprächs Notizen gemacht werden. Die entsprechenden Spalten des Vordrucks für den Vermerk sind korrekt auszufüllen. Bei den Angaben zum ausländischen Gesprächspartner darf der Name der Firma nicht fehlen. Wenn möglich, sind auch die Stadt und das Land anzugeben. Die Rubrik **Betrifft** muss unbedingt ausgefüllt werden. Der Hinweis **Dringend** kann erforderlich sein. Der Vermerk soll alle wichtigen Angaben (Fakten, Namen, Zahlen, Daten) enthalten und so vollständig sein, dass er auch Dritten, die mit der Angelegenheit nicht vertraut sind, später als Handlungsgrundlage dienen kann. Aus diesem Grund muss alles Wichtige, das der deutsche Gesprächspartner sagt, ebenfalls in den Vermerk eingearbeitet werden. Unwichtiges und Überflüssiges sollte nicht wiedergegeben werden. Für Verstöße gegen die Regeln der deutschen Grammatik, Rechtschreibung und Zeichensetzung werden Punkte abgezogen. Deutsch ist Prüfungssprache. Indirekte Rede im Konjunktiv ist nicht erforderlich. Ein allgemeines zweisprachiges Wörterbuch darf benutzt werden. Ein Vermerk hat in der Regel keine förmliche Anrede und Grußformel.

4 Vermerk über einen Geschäftsbrief

§2 (2) d) der Rechtsvorschriften – Richtzeit: 30 Minuten

Die Prüfungsteilnehmer erhalten eine Situationsbeschreibung mit Aufgabe sowie eine schriftliche Geschäftskorrespondenz, über die sie einen zusammenfassenden Vermerk für einen Dritten erstellen müssen. Beim Ausfüllen des Vordrucks ist zu beachten, dass, abgesehen von den Angaben zu Verfasser/-in und Empfänger/-in des Vermerks, dem Datum und dem Namen des Verfassers des Geschäftsbriefs, wenn möglich auch dessen Position angegeben werden sollte, sowie Name und Anschrift (Ort und Land) der Firma. Unter der Rubrik **Betrifft** ist der Hauptgegenstand des Briefes zu nennen. Der vorgelegte Geschäftsbrief darf nicht übersetzt werden, sondern muss unter Einbeziehung aller wichtigen Informationen so zusammengefasst werden, dass er – wie der Telefonvermerk – auch Dritten, die mit der Angelegenheit nicht vertraut sind, später als Handlungsgrundlage dienen kann. Belanglose, wiederholte oder rein füllende Aussagen sollten weggelassen werden, da in der Praxis ein knapper Vermerk, der jedoch alles Wesentliche enthält, einer weitschweifigen Inhaltsangabe vorzuziehen ist. Die Beherrschung der deutschen Sprache ist auch hier ein Bewertungskriterium. Ein allgemeines, zweisprachiges Wörterbuch darf benutzt werden.

5 Nachweis der Fremdsprachenbeherrschung durch einen Sprachergänzungstest

§2 (2) e) der Rechtsvorschrift – Bearbeitungszeit: 25 Minuten

Es darf **kein** Wörterbuch benutzt werden. Der Test umfasst zwei Lückentexte. Mit Text 1 wird die Beherrschung des kaufmännischen Wortschatzes und der Redewendungen getestet. 20 der 23 angegebenen Wörter sind in die Lücken einzusetzen. Text 2 dient der Überprüfung der Kenntnisse grammatischer Strukturen und Präpositionen. Von je drei Alternativen pro Lücke ist die jeweils korrekte in eine der 30 Lücken einzusetzen. Gerade dieser Prüfungsteil bedarf wiederholter, intensiver Übung.

Mündliche Prüfung

1 Gespräch in der Fremdsprache – Unterhaltung über Themen des Ausbildungsbereichs und Rollenspiel

§ 2 (3) b) der Rechtsvorschrift – Dauer der mündlichen Prüfung ca. 20 Minuten

Bei der Unterhaltung mit einem Prüfer / einer Prüferin **(Teil 1)** z. B. über den Ausbildungsbetrieb, die durchlaufenen Abteilungen und die Berufsschule kommt es in erster Linie auf die gelungene Kommunikation an, erst in zweiter Linie auf sprachliche Korrektheit. Mit dem Rollenspiel **(Teil 2)** (z. B. Empfang eines Besuchers) soll die Fähigkeit zur fremdsprachlichen Bewältigung häufig auftretender Alltagssituationen nachgewiesen werden. Es darf **kein** Wörterbuch benutzt werden.

2 Telefongespräch geschäftlicher Natur in der Fremdsprache

§ 2 (3) a) der Rechtsvorschrift – Dauer der mündlichen Prüfung ca. 20 Minuten

Die zu prüfende Person erhält schriftliche Angaben in Deutsch zu einem Geschäftsfall und darf sich einige Minuten schriftlich auf das Telefongespräch vorbereiten, das er / sie mit einem Prüfer / einer Prüferin führen wird. Es empfiehlt sich dabei, lediglich leicht lesbare Stichworte niederzuschreiben. Auch bei diesem Prüfungsteil ist vor allem die erfolgreiche Kommunikation wichtig, d.h. die Brauchbarkeit des Telefonats für die Praxis sowie die Beherrschung der gängigen Telefonredewendungen. Es darf **kein** Wörterbuch benutzt werden.

Teil 1 Gespräch in der Fremdsprache

§2 (3) b) der Rechtsvorschriften

Unterhaltung über Themen des Ausbildungsbereichs

Eine/-r der drei Prüfer/-innen beginnt die Unterhaltung mit dem Prüfling etwa wie folgt:

- Good morning / afternoon …
- Could you introduce yourself, please?
- Where do you live?
- Where are you doing your traineeship?
- How long have you been working for …?
- When did you start your training?
- When does it finish?

Darauf könnte ein Gespräch über die Firma folgen:

- Could you describe your firm?
- What are its main products or services?
- Is it a manufacturer or a services company?
- How many people does it employ roughly?
- Does it have subsidiaries or branches?
- Where are its main markets – domestic, EU or overseas?
- How well is this particular sector doing at the present time?

Fragen zur Ausbildung im engeren Sinne kommen auch häufig vor:

- Where are you attending vocational school?
- Are you on block release or do you attend school one day a week?
- What are your favourite subjects?
- Do you find vocational school useful in your work?
- Could you tell us more about your work? Which departments have you worked in?
- Which did you prefer? Was there any department you didn't like?
- Could you describe your daily routine?
- How in your opinion could the training in your company be improved?*
- Could you describe the dual system of vocational training in Germany?*
- When are you going to sit your final exam? What will be the main subjects?
- What field would you like to work in when you have completed your training?

* Themen für besonders gute Kandidaten / Kandidatinnen

Einige allgemeine Themen könnten ebenfalls angesprochen werden:

- What are your plans for the future (work, further training, travel)?
- Have you ever been to the UK or USA or another English-speaking country?
- Could you describe your impressions?
- Are you interested in music or sport?
- What are your hobbies?

Das Gespräch in der Fremdsprache soll jedoch eine echte Unterhaltung sein, kein Frage- und Antwortspiel. In erster Linie kommt es auf die gelungene Kommunikation an, erst in zweiter Linie auf sprachliche Korrektheit.

Teil 2 Bewältigung häufig auftretender Alltagssituationen

§2 (2) b) der Rechtsvorschriften

Die Fähigkeit zur Bewältigung häufig auftretender Alltagssituationen wird in einem Rollenspiel nachgewiesen. Es könnte etwa wie folgt aussehen: Ein/-e Prüfer/-in spielt beispielsweise eine/-n Besucher/-in aus dem Ausland, der / die einen Termin mit dem Vorgesetzten / der Vorgesetzten des Prüflings hat, aber etwas zu früh kommt. Oder der Vorgesetzte steckt im Stau und wird voraussichtlich ca. 15 Minuten Verspätung haben. Vom Prüfling wird erwartet, dass er / sie sich um den Besucher kümmert:

- Good morning, Mr / Mrs / Miss / Ms X
- I'm afraid Mr X is still in a meeting. He'll be finished in about 10 minutes' time / Mr X has rung to say he's stuck in traffic and will be here in about 15 minutes.
- May I take your coat / umbrella?
- Did you have a good journey? / How was your flight?
- Would you like to make yourself comfortable here until Mr X arrives?
- Would you perhaps like some tea or coffee?
- Would you like milk or lemon with the tea?
- Perhaps you'd like to look at the Financial Times or our company brochure while you're waiting.

Weitere mögliche small talk-Themen:

- The weather here and where the visitor has come from
- Hotel accommodation
- Local public transport
- Local and regional attractions
- Local food and drink
- Current events – e.g. carnival, football matches, tennis tournament etc.
- Where to spend the evening (restaurants / pubs / concerts / musicals)
- How to get to main station / exhibition centre / airport / town centre

Andere denkbare Situationen könnten Verkaufsgespräche oder eine Kundenberatung sein, die zum Arbeitsgebiet der zu prüfenden Person gehören.

Incoterms® 2020

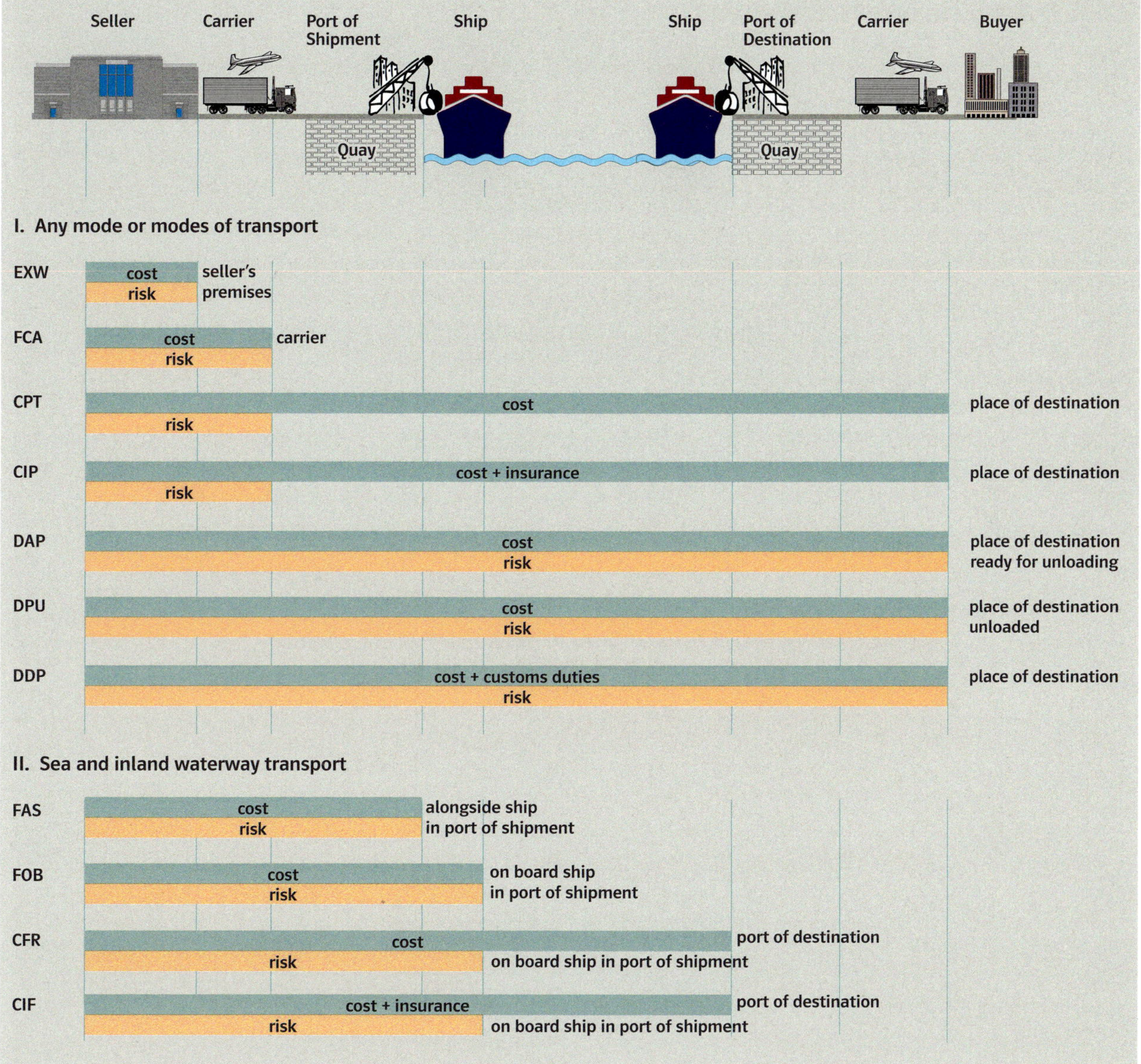

Quellennachweis

8 Getty Images Plus, München (E+/Cecilie_Arcurs); **9** ShutterStock.com RF, New York (GoodStudio); **12** Getty Images Plus, München (E+/cokada); **16** ShutterStock.com RF, New York (ivector); **17** ShutterStock.com RF, New York (Dilen); **18** ShutterStock.com RF, New York (SasinTipchai); **24** Getty Images, München (Westend61); **30** ShutterStock.com RF, New York (r.classen); **36** Getty Images Plus, München (E+/svetikd); **44** Getty Images Plus, München (iStock/kynny); **48.1** ShutterStock.com RF, New York (Funtap); **48.2** iStockphoto, Calgary, Alberta (Jay Lazarin); **48.3** stock.adobe.com, Dublin (Acnaleksy); **48.4** ShutterStock.com RF, New York (Pierre-Yves Babelon); **48.5** stock.adobe.com, Dublin (EvrenKalinbacak); **50.1** ShutterStock.com RF, New York (Grigvovan); **50.2** ShutterStock.com RF, New York (Kzenon); **51.1** ShutterStock.com RF, New York (Good Shop Background); **51.2** ShutterStock.com RF, New York (Zay Nyi Nyi); **51.3** ShutterStock.com RF, New York (Drew300); **51.4** ShutterStock.com RF, New York (MUSTAFA HAMDIEV); **51.5** ShutterStock.com RF, New York (sirikorn thamniyom); **51.6** ShutterStock.com RF, New York (Nikola Obradovic); **51.7** ShutterStock.com RF, New York (Skocko); **51.8** ShutterStock.com RF, New York (Travis Klein); **54** ShutterStock.com RF, New York (Es sarawuth); **57** stock.adobe.com, Dublin (Photographee.eu); **60** ShutterStock.com RF, New York (PopTika); **61** ShutterStock.com RF, New York (Tond Van Graphcraft); **62** stock.adobe.com, Dublin (jenny on the moon); **65** ShutterStock.com RF, New York (Tond Van Graphcraft); **67** Getty Images Plus, München (iStock/kadmy); **69** ShutterStock.com RF, New York (vinap); **72** Getty Images, München (Westend61); **74** ShutterStock.com RF, New York (B illustrations); **84** ShutterStock.com RF, New York (Monkey Business Images); **91** ShutterStock.com RF, New York (TeraVector); **98** Getty Images Plus, München (E+/SolStock); **100** ShutterStock.com RF, New York (Nomad_Soul); **102** ShutterStock.com RF, New York (Alexander Dobrikov); **104** ShutterStock.com RF, New York (r.classen); **106.1-3** Satzkiste GmbH, Stuttgart; **110** stock.adobe.com, Dublin (Andrey Popov); **111.1** ShutterStock.com RF, New York (CreativeX Studio); **111.2** ShutterStock.com RF, New York (madpixblue); **113** stock.adobe.com, Dublin (detailblick-foto); **127** JupiterImages photos.com, Tucson, AZ (clipart.com); **Umschlag** stock.adobe.com, Dublin (nutawut)